BOWL with BRYANT

To my wife Ruth whose
encouragement,
understanding and loyal
support helped to make it
all possible.

WILLOW BOOKS
Collins
8 Grafton Street, London W1
1989

This book is based on material from Bowls International magazine, supplemented and updated.

Produced for Willow Books, 8 Grafton Street, London, W1X 3LA, by Key Publishing Ltd, P.O. Box 100, Stamford, Lincolnshire, PE9 1XQ. Printed by Hazell Watson and Viney Limited, Aylesbury, Bucks. Colour process by Publishers Reprographic Services Ltd., 4 Roger Street, London WC1. Typeset and composed by Arty Type, Whittlesey, Peterborough.

Willow Books
William Collins Sons & Co Ltd
London ● Glasgow ● Sydney ● Auckland
Toronto ● Johannesburg.

First published 1984; fifth impression 1989
Bryant, David, 19—
Bowl with Bryant.
1. Bowling on the green
I. Title
796.31   GV909
ISBN 0 00 218025 1

Foreword

Jimmy Davidson is Secretary of the World Indoor Bowls Council, England's National Coach and a former English Bowls Association singles champion.

IT IS REASONABLE to claim, and I would argue the point with all the fervour of the 'sports-mad', that in a period which so far covers more than two decades, David Bryant CBE has dominated his chosen sport more than any other sportsman in the world.

Fortunately for readers of this book David Bryant the Bowler has a facility, remarkable among top class sportsmen, for communicating with rare clarity and insight full details of the knowledge and skills which have taken him to the very summit and kept him there.

Having read, and learned, from this book in the serial form in which it first appeared in 'Bowls International' magazine, I am confident that bowlers will find very precise answers to their problems as a result of David unselfishly imparting knowledge and wisdom acquired in the unique achievements of his career as the first Superstar of Bowls.

But it is not David's personal bowling achievements I wish to draw attention to in this foreword, but Bryant the Coach. When the English Bowls Coaching Scheme was first being introduced in 1979, it was suggested to me that its task was to produce the first ever English bowls coaches. I maintained, and still do, that bowls coaches, good and bad, had existed ever since bowls was first played as pairs, triples and fours – except that they were called skips who gave skilled and unskilled practical coaching to their team members.

David's record as a skip at national, international and world level bears ample testimony to his practical ability as an eminently successful coach, even when applied during the pressure of competition at the very highest level.

I quote two very different examples based on personal observation. The first was in Australia watching David 'nurse' the precocious talent of young Jimmy Hobday and Tony Allcock, now both bowls stars in their own right, through ten days of fierce competition to the effect that all three performed throughout at concert pitch to win the 1980 World Triples Championship. (Incidentally, I also had the rare privilege between games, and occasionally between ends, of hearing David coaching himself to the 1980 World Singles Championship).

The second, at a lower level of competition in England, was to watch him restore the confidence of a temporarily struggling member of his four. For several ends David brought the player on to the same hand at drawing weight even when it seemed the 'wrong' shot according to requirements of the head. Improved performance by the player in the last crucial ends of the game was the reward for sound, inobtrusive, practical coaching by Bryant the skip and coach.

Not many bowlers can enjoy the good fortune of practical coaching as a playing member of a Bryant four. A great many more will undoubtedly benefit from attending one of David's coaching courses and more will have learned from watching him in action. However, every bowler, man and woman, now has the opportunity, through reading this book once, to improve personal standards of performance. But to read it once would be a gross misuse of new, first-class, do-it-yourself bowls coaching material.

My advice to bowlers at every level, from raw beginner to experienced international, would be to use the book as a continuous source of reference and inspiration. I know I will – I only regret that I did not have it as a personal manual of guidance when I first started playing forty-plus years ago.

3

Contents

EXPERIENCE

TEMPERAMENT

Acknowledgement: Invaluable assistance in the compilation of this book was given by
Bowls International magazine staff members Chris Mills (editor), Duncan Cubitt
(photographer) and Bob Warters (publisher).

Introduction

TO THE average person there is apparently nothing difficult about the game of bowls. But bowling to me is an art, a science and the subject of a lifetime. You might exhaust yourself – but never your subject.

Bowls is a game that calls for skill, strategy and self control. It is a great revealer of character.

Some shots in the game are amazingly simple in their execution, others more complex. But whatever the shot, knowing what to do and how to play it to the required situation are all important for any bowler who wishes to succeed.

This book is designed to show the art of bowling. It covers all stages of the game, giving hints that can help players of all levels.

Although I had the benefit early on in my career from many bowlers, including my late father Reg, I was nevertheless largely self-taught. In today's world, players have the advantage of the National Coaching Scheme. My course is complementary to this body's teachings, but I will be adding the tips and expertise of bowls played my way.

The art of bowling can be divided into four main sections – mechanics, concentration, experience and temperament. Within these broad guidelines are many sub-sections, which I will cover step-by-step with a positive analysis of all the points that go into the making of these skills.

And it is not just enough to show how – you must always explain why.

Like most sports, even the most experienced players are still learning. A good player must always be prepared to undergo self-assessment and learn from others.

Firstly we shall deal with the **Mechanics** of the game. Delivery, for example, will investigate the choice of bowl, grips, stance and how to establish good line and length. The battery of shots at a bowler's disposal will be discussed, along with how physical fitness can play a part.

The ability to concentrate is a vital stage in development of play and so **Concentration** forms our second main section. How to make a study of the green in terms of pace and condition, tactics and teamwork – all fall into this area. Decisions have to be made, such as which hand and which shot. In these situations you must be able to analyse what will be gained if you succeed – and what might be lost if you fail.

Our third section is **Experience,** something that can only fully evolve with time but can be accelerated to some extent. Here I will be passing on my knowledge of all types of surfaces, and how to adapt your play in each case. With experience comes self-discipline, coolness under pressure, confidence and the ability to shut out all distractions.

Finally, we will look at **Temperament.** Determination to succeed is a good thing, but the bowler must also be a good team member and show sportsmanship. I'll deal with ways of improving your approach to a match, how to handle other players and the question of etiquette.

Enjoy the book. I hope it makes you a champion too.

David J. Bryant.

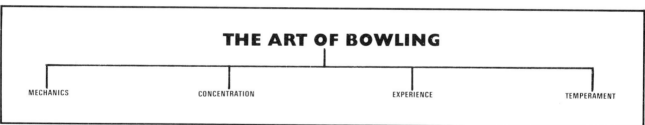

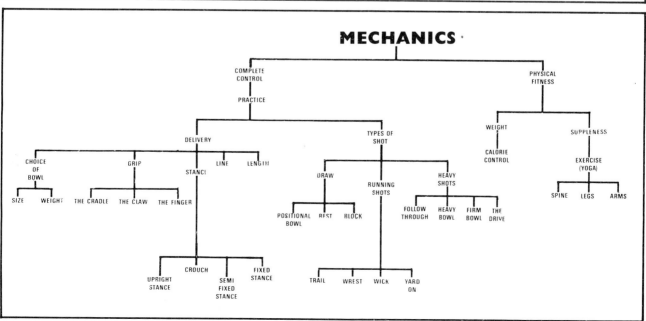

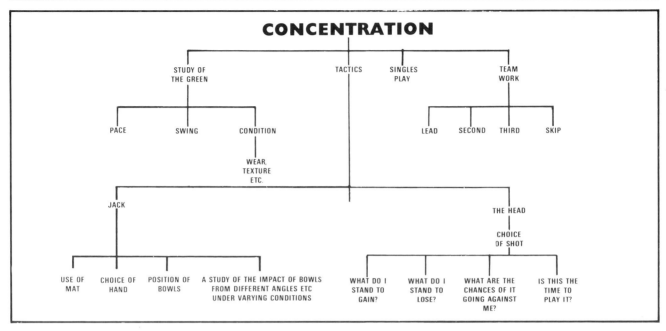

CONCENTRATION

STUDY OF THE GREEN — TACTICS — SINGLES PLAY — TEAM WORK

STUDY OF THE GREEN: PACE, SWING, CONDITION

CONDITION: WEAR, TEXTURE ETC.

TEAM WORK: LEAD, SECOND, THIRD, SKIP

TACTICS: JACK — THE HEAD

THE HEAD: CHOICE OF SHOT

JACK: USE OF MAT, CHOICE OF HAND, POSITION OF BOWLS, A STUDY OF THE IMPACT OF BOWLS FROM DIFFERENT ANGLES ETC UNDER VARYING CONDITIONS

CHOICE OF SHOT: WHAT DO I STAND TO GAIN?, WHAT DO I STAND TO LOSE?, WHAT ARE THE CHANCES OF IT GOING AGAINST ME?, IS THIS THE TIME TO PLAY IT?

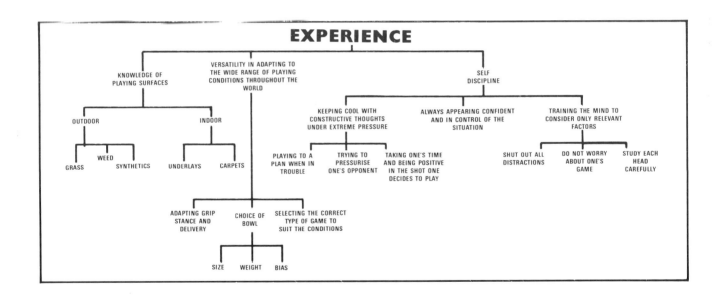

EXPERIENCE

KNOWLEDGE OF PLAYING SURFACES — VERSATILITY IN ADAPTING TO THE WIDE RANGE OF PLAYING CONDITIONS THROUGHOUT THE WORLD — SELF DISCIPLINE

KNOWLEDGE OF PLAYING SURFACES: OUTDOOR, INDOOR

OUTDOOR: GRASS, WEED, SYNTHETICS

INDOOR: UNDERLAYS, CARPETS

VERSATILITY: ADAPTING GRIP STANCE AND DELIVERY, CHOICE OF BOWL, SELECTING THE CORRECT TYPE OF GAME TO SUIT THE CONDITIONS

CHOICE OF BOWL: SIZE, WEIGHT, BIAS

SELF DISCIPLINE: KEEPING COOL WITH CONSTRUCTIVE THOUGHTS UNDER EXTREME PRESSURE, ALWAYS APPEARING CONFIDENT AND IN CONTROL OF THE SITUATION, TRAINING THE MIND TO CONSIDER ONLY RELEVANT FACTORS

KEEPING COOL: PLAYING TO A PLAN WHEN IN TROUBLE, TRYING TO PRESSURISE ONE'S OPPONENT, TAKING ONE'S TIME AND BEING POSITIVE IN THE SHOT ONE DECIDES TO PLAY

TRAINING THE MIND: SHUT OUT ALL DISTRACTIONS, DO NOT WORRY ABOUT ONE'S GAME, STUDY EACH HEAD CAREFULLY

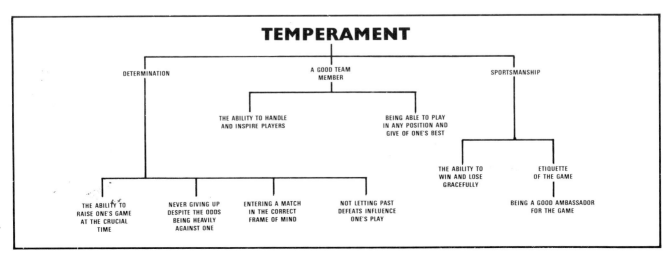

TEMPERAMENT

DETERMINATION — A GOOD TEAM MEMBER — SPORTSMANSHIP

A GOOD TEAM MEMBER: THE ABILITY TO HANDLE AND INSPIRE PLAYERS, BEING ABLE TO PLAY IN ANY POSITION AND GIVE OF ONE'S BEST

DETERMINATION: THE ABILITY TO RAISE ONE'S GAME AT THE CRUCIAL TIME, NEVER GIVING UP DESPITE THE ODDS BEING HEAVILY AGAINST ONE, ENTERING A MATCH IN THE CORRECT FRAME OF MIND, NOT LETTING PAST DEFEATS INFLUENCE ONE'S PLAY

SPORTSMANSHIP: THE ABILITY TO WIN AND LOSE GRACEFULLY, ETIQUETTE OF THE GAME

ETIQUETTE OF THE GAME: BEING A GOOD AMBASSADOR FOR THE GAME

Choice of bowls

Determine size, weight, type for best effect

Each sport has its own individual equipment and for a bowler to execute his skills he will rely on a set of bowls. So choosing the right set is all important.

Many bowlers will keep the one set throughout their playing careers, although nowadays it's not that unusual for top class bowlers to have more than one set, using them under differing conditions.

I do not intend to make the choice for players. I use **Drakelite** for reasons which should become apparent as I develop my theories and methods.

But really it is up to each bowler to discover which type of bowl suits him best.

I am often asked – 'How do you set about choosing a bowl?'

Many text books suggest that you get hold of a manufacturer's gauge, which shows you what size to have depending largely on the size of your hand, or span the circumference of the bowl with both hands. The largest bowl suitable is the one where the tips of the middle fingers just meet. These are two orthodox methods but let me say right away that I disagree!

I have always used bowls that are bigger than those indicated by a gauge. In fact they are nearly a quarter-of-an-inch 'too big'. This is because I prefer a bowl which slides easily out of my hand.

There is always the danger that the bowler may have problems in wet weather, but under most conditions the extra weight given by the bigger size bowl is a great advantage.

I know that the changing of the 'weight-for-size' rule has given players with smaller hands a chance to reverse this advantage considerably, but I still prefer the larger bowl. But firstly we are talking about choice of bowl, so here are the main types available:– **Taylor-Rolph:** (Wisden-Edwards): Manufacture the new 'Concorde' bowl but perhaps are still better known for the 'Tyrolite' bowl, which is used by England international, Mal Hughes. **Henselite:** Manufactured in Australia and used by most of the players in the 1980 World Men's Bowls Championships. Takes a fairly wide sweep and curves nicely at the end of its run. **Thomas Taylor's:** A very famous name in Glasgow. Taylor's produce bowls both for flat and crown green bowlers and the 'Lignoid' trademark is very popular. **Vitalite:** Another of the British-produced bowls which is popular with many club bowlers. They are made by the same company that produce top-class billiard, snooker and pool balls.

First flat green bowl from crown green specialists A F Ayers is the Greenmaster, introduced in 1983.

You can have all of the above bowls with or without a grip. This grip will help some bowlers who really like to feel their bowl.

I began my bowling career using 'lignums' but I think we can accept that most bowlers these days will use composition bowls. I obtained my first set of composition bowls in 1952.

There are two types of bowl – the British and Australian. The British manufactured bowl takes what I would describe as a 'banana' arc to the jack. With the Australian bowl the line is not so pronounced but it draws into the head more as it slows down.

I would also say that this type of bowl will ride out the bumps of an outdoor green or the little tricks to be found on some indoor carpets better than most bowls.

Combining the best features of both types would obviously produce a bowl suitable for all conditions and it was for this reason that Drakelite Ltd and Thos' Taylor of Glasgow teamed up several years ago. After considerable research and effort the revolutionary Drakelite bowl was released to the market in the Spring of 1983. The appearance is pleasing to the eye but what is far more important is the material which is far easier to grip in adverse weather conditions.

The three things any potential purchaser must determine when choosing a set of bowls are – SIZE, TYPE and what ARC he would like.

The sizes for bowls are now numbered from 0 to 7 (ie: 4⅝

David Bryant linked with Thomas Taylor Ltd to produce his own bowl, Bryant's Drakelite.

Widely used by many players are Vitalite (above), the distinctive Concorde (left) and Australian-made Henselite. Every player has to discover which type suits them best though it is becoming more common to have two or even three sets for different conditions.

Choice of bowls

Drakes Pride bowls come from E A Clare and were computer-developed with the aid of students at Liverpool University.

inch to 5⅛ inch). The types are those that I have listed. The last criteria, the arc, is the most difficult to measure. In fact, it's impossible to determine until you have played with them.

It is one of those unfortunate things that you cannot know what amount of swing a bowl will have until it is used. You can take three sets of a certain type of bowl, all the same size, and I can guarantee that they will take a slightly different arc to the jack. And this is even allowing for the fact that they are stamped 'standard three bias'.

I think a player will learn a lot more about the game with a bowl that takes a wider arc to the jack, but then there are occasions when a bowl that takes a narrower line can be quite useful. The bowl that takes a wider arc will create good habits because they need to be 'bowled'.

Ideally a new player coming into the game should borrow a few sets to try out until he finds one that suits him best.

If you are going to make a capital outlay of between £70 and £125 it's best to try and get it right first time.

But if any bowler finds he cannot manage with a particular set – don't continue, change them!

It is therefore important that a player should end up with the bowl that he feels most comfortable with.

With the choice of bowl a lot may depend on the type of hand the bowler has. The length of your fingers and width of palm will often determine the right size. But for people taking up the game in the British Isles I would recommend choosing the largest size that can be comfortably handled. The most important thing to remember is that the length of the fingers is really the main factor in being able to propel a bowl successfully. I use a Drakelite 5 1/16. Perhaps with the same size in the older type wooden 'lignums' I would find it a bit of a struggle as they have a much wider running track. I would feel that it was difficult to encompass the bowl.

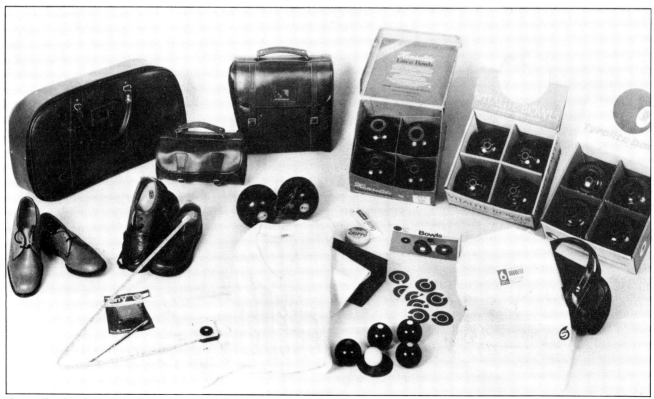

A small selection of equipment and clothing available for the bowls enthusiast.

The days of the 'round' bowl are nearly over and you will find most bowls used today are more elliptical in shape.

I think that when a player is selecting what to buy he should also consider what materials suit him best because different makes have different surfaces. Some have what I would term a 'glassy' finish and I find these difficult to grip because I have a moist hand.

This can of course be remedied by the use of a wax polish but bowlers with dry hands will not want to bother to use a wax.

It is possible to bowl with a larger size on indoor surfaces where you don't encounter any wet conditions and there is less drag on the surface.

If you choose a bowl of 5 inches or more, which I think would be the majority of men, I don't think the heavyweight bowl gives that much advantage. But in the smaller sizes, and I am thinking here more of lady bowlers, the heavyweight bowl could well help.

It is very important that a bowler, particularly someone just coming into the game, should not have a bowl that is too large. You mustn't feel that it is difficult to hold it. The bowl must feel relaxed in your hand.

If you are struggling to span the bowl with your fingers, your hand feels tense, your muscles are tense and this will affect your delivery.

It is a case that firstly the bowl must not slip out of your hand and secondly it feels comfortable across the width of your palm.

You mustn't feel any tension in your hand at all.

To some degree the size can be affected by the grip you adopt. So having chosen a particular bowl the next step is to discover the best way of holding (or gripping) that bowl for delivery.

Becoming far rarer are bowls like these made from the hard wood lignum vitae, now giving way to synthetic composition material in mass manufacture.

Bowls on the test bench being checked for consistency of line.

Grip

Claw or cradle – choosing a grip to suit you

In bowls there are basically three ways of gripping the bowl for delivery – the **claw**, the **cradle** and the **finger**.

At the extreme end of the cradle, the bowl is gripped very tightly by the tips of the fingers and the thumb. Moving back from this point, more and more of the fingers and finally the palm of the hand make contact. The thumb rests comfortably on the side as does the little finger but obviously to a lesser extent. The bowl rests in the 'cradle' formed by the palm and the fingers.

The claw grip is undoubtedly the most widely used as it is suitable for all conditions. The bowl is held exactly the same as for the cradle but the thumb is placed on or slightly inside the large ring which in turn raises the bowl off the palm of the hand giving a far more sensitive touch.

The cradle grip is used predominantly in the Northern Hemisphere where the greens are much slower and is rarely, if ever, seen on the faster surfaces of Australia and New Zealand.

The bowl is cradled in the palm of the hand with the thumb acting as a prop approximately in the centre of the small circle or disc.

This grip has proved successful on the majority of greens but cannot be recommended on the very fast surfaces as the bowl is palmed away, making it extremely difficult to obtain the delicate touch needed under conditions similar to those found in the Southern Hemisphere.

A lot of people use the cradle grip because they can bowl with a bigger bowl than with the claw grip. They have more of the hand to work with and haven't got to bring the thumb over the top. If you have a short thumb, you can't get it over the top and might need a smaller bowl.

Hands are funny things. You get some people with small thumbs and long fingers and some people with long thumbs and stubby fingers. If you look at most people's hands you will find that their second and first fingers are different lengths. That is why I take the weight of the bowl between the second and third fingers – most people take the weight on the second finger.

In all cases the middle (or longest) finger makes a line with the forearm and this will continue through the bowl when it is held in the upright position. That is with its greater diameter in a vertical plane, unless the bowler is deliberately introducing a tilt.

If the bowl is not held properly, you will develop bad habits. The bowl will not leave the hand properly and smoothly, and could be bumped or scooped. It will not leave the hand along the intended line of direction and even if it does, a bowl not launched on an even keel will have deviated from the intended line when it reaches the end of its run.

I have tried various grips during my career and nowadays use one grip for all shots. Where I differ is in varying the pressures I apply according to the particular demands of a shot and the pace of the green.

With my own grip my thumb is well over the top of the

Above: Note how in this shot taken on the faster indoor surface at Coatbridge, the thumb is near the top of the bowl to aid the more delicate touch required in delivery.

Right: Using the free hand to steady the bowl, make sure the bowling fingers are parallel to the running surface at ALL times.

This is not wrong, of course, but in my opinion it is not absolutely essential.

I am a firm believer that it doesn't really matter if your fingers are evenly placed over the running surface, with the second finger down the middle of the bowl to take the weight of the bowl, or slightly to one side as mine always are. It is up to the individual as long as he remembers to keep them parallel.

If the fingers are slightly across the running surface – it will create a wobble on the bowl. And with the modern, more 'upright' bowls this will be more pronounced.

The reason why I have my fingers slightly to one side are because of the position of the little finger.

The little finger is not much use to a bowler. Where do you put it? If you take the weight on the second finger as most people recommend, it is almost certain that the little finger would find its way round to the side of the bowl. On a forehand shot it would be on the bias side.

And if it comes round to the side of the bowl it is an immediate danger because if it comes into play at the moment of delivery it can again cause a bowl to wobble.

It comes more into play when a bowler adopts the cradle type delivery because the bowl then sits in the palm of the hand with the palm acting like a cup. The bowl is then rolled away rather than delivered.

The claw is in my opinion the best and only grip for use on all types of surface.

Most people will have their bowl in an upright position when it leaves their hand, mine are very slightly tilted – inwards for a forehand shot and outwards for a backhand delivery. But this is just one of the little points I have perfected over my long bowling career.

There is a slight variation to the standard claw grip that I adopt on occasions, called the 'finger-grip'. The bowl comes more forward, the thumb more to the top. This will be used more on a very fast green where the bowl is only 'stroked' up the green.

So get your grip right. It's very important.

Some points to remember...
THE GRIP

(1) Fingers must be parallel to the running surface of the bowl at all times.
(2) Watch the little finger!
(3) Vary the pressure of the grip to suit the speed of the green.
(4) When holding the bowl the grip should be tension free. It must feel comfortable in the hand.
(5) Do not cup the bowl. If held correctly it will not slip.
(6) Players with very small hands or short thumbs may have to adopt the cradle grip.

bowl though not right over it, and my fingers are slightly more widely spread than with the normal claw.

Whether I am bowling a forehand or backhand shot, the bowl will definitely be in my fingers rather than on the palm of my hand.

It is in my fingers that I get the 'feel'.

There is always the danger with finger-grips of skidding the bowl away, but I am always careful to make sure that the bowl rolls out of my fingers. There is a tendency to push, but there will be no skid on the bowl. To help this I have exaggerated my follow-through.

It is most important that the player does not over-grip the bowl. Grip tension will cause problems.

The most important factor about grip and delivery is that when the bowl goes down on to the green it goes down in an identical manner every time.

It is therefore most important that the fingers should be parallel to the running base of the bowl at ALL times.

All the coaching manuals that I have read, and indeed most of the experts, say that the second (or middle) finger should be placed along the middle of the running surface.

Grip

THE CRADLE

For the cradle grip, the bowl nestles in the palm of the hand with the thumb angled slightly upwards . . .

THE CLAW

The bowl comes forward out of the palm and rests on the fingers for the claw grip and the thumb moves to the region of the rings . . .

THE FINGER

Not so much used in Britain where the slower greens require a firmer grip . . .

. . . the little finger is slightly spread to form the cradle . . .

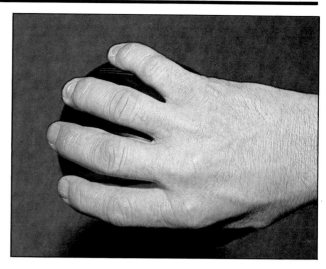

. . . and the fingers should be evenly spread to be parallel to the running base of the bowl.

. . . this moves the little finger lower in the grip . . .

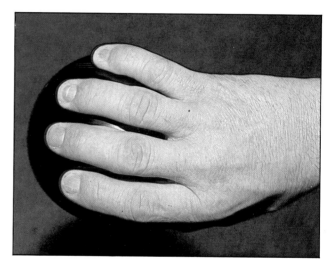

. . . and the rest of the fingers are much closer together, but still parallel to the running base of the bowl.

. . . the finger grip is more popular in Australia and New Zealand, with the thumb resting just inside the rings . . .

. . . and the bowl more forward in the fingers, achieves more sensitivity on the faster greens.

Stance and delivery

FROM THE FRONT...

THE body moves rhythmically down the aiming line with a smooth flowing action and during delivery the shoulder, forearm, wrist and bowl should all stay in line.

1

2

5

4

3

AND FROM THE REAR

DON'T allow the right elbow to stray from the side of the body as this will cause a hooked delivery ... and don't lift your head until the bowl is grounded.

1

2

4

5

...FROM THE SIDE

NOTE how during delivery the bodyweight is transferred from right foot to left foot – with the left hand acting as a prop on the left thigh to enable a smooth action.

2

1

4

5

Stance and delivery

FOUR STYLES ON THE MAT . . .

The fixed . . . The player gets into this static position before swinging his arm through to the aiming point.

The Athletic . . . The most popular stance with bodyweight evenly balanced on both feet before stepping off the mat.

The crouch . . . Bryant's personal choice of stance, he says, enables him to maintain a more accurate line.

The semi-fixed . . . as used by many South Africans with the player stepping partly forward before completing the step on delivery.

How to establish a smooth, regular action

It's as well to remember that the first step towards successful bowling is perfecting your delivery. It is also important to recognise that delivery is not one distinct action.

Delivery takes in everything that you do from the moment you pick up your bowl and step on the mat to the point where your bowl is halfway up the green.

It is basically in four functions – grip, stance, delivery and follow through.

As with other aspects of the game, the position a player adopts on the mat – his stance – is a matter of personal preference. There is only one law which must be followed and that is that at the moment of delivery, when the bowl touches the surface of play, at least all of one foot must be either on the mat or directly above it (that is entirely within the confines of the mat).

More experienced bowlers will work out what they feel is their best position on the mat, but for beginners it is best to start by standing in the centre with feet parallel, a few inches apart, pointing along the line that your bowl is going to take.

In all sports where an object has to be rolled, bowled, thrown or struck – the motive force should be generated more by weight transfer than by arm movement. In general terms the arm is a partly contributory vehicle.

Bowls is not a game that demands violent physical actions, but it is important that your delivery must be conditioned to ensure a smooth and accurate line for your bowl, with good distribution of forces on the muscles that will be used.

Basically there are four stances that can be adopted for delivery – the athletic, the crouch, the fixed and semi-fixed.

The **ATHLETIC STANCE**, also known as the upright stance, is easily the most popular and is seen on greens throughout the world. It certainly proves an advantage on slower greens as it is far easier to impart more force behind the bowl from this position and still maintain accuracy.

My delivery stems from the relaxed positition of the arm (left), which when it hangs by your side causes the palm to face inwards. In fact it is only possible to take the arm back in a perfectly straight line, while keeping the body square to the aiming line by using a full 180 degree turn of the palm at the top of the backswing (below). The main advantage is the relaxed, tension free arm action which must aid better weight control.

Stance and delivery

1

The **CROUCH STANCE,** although nowhere near as common as the athletic, is generally accepted as an alternative and is used by quite a number of players. I personally adopt this stance and believe it enables me to maintain a more accurate line. The degree of crouch naturally varies from player to player and also with the pace of the green. My own style is the full crouch with legs fully bent, the body weight being taken on the back of the legs.

I find I can hold this position for as long as I like without the discomfort I would experience from a semi-crouch stance. All bowlers are vulnerable to fatigue in the calf muscles, particularly on fast greens where the speed of the action is greatly reduced.

The **FIXED STANCE,** so called because the front foot is

2

placed down the delivery line, is the least used but is often adopted by bowlers with a physical disability as it is the most comfortable way for them to ground the bowl. As the step has already been taken the free hand stabilises the body by grasping the thigh or knee of the front leg. It obviously has its limitations and I would not personally recommend it, but having said that, there are many fine bowlers who use this method. It is a personal choice as other factors such as a player's height, weight, reach and length have to be considered.

The **SEMI-FIXED STANCE** is a cross between the athletic stance and the fixed stance as the front foot is moved partly down the delivery line when the player takes his position on the mat. During the delivery the front foot moves forward to complete the step. The main merit of this particular stance is selection of the delivery line by the front foot in the initial stage. This must surely minimise error in missing the correct line and a higher percentage of well greened bowls should be grassed. As in the fixed stance, the body is stabilised by the free hand grasping the thigh or knee of the front leg.

The main criteria is that the bowler feels comfortable and at ease on the mat. The feet should be sufficiently apart to give a good balance, the knees relaxed and the bodyweight slightly forward. The bowl should be held firmly but without tension in the wrist or arm.

As the name obviously indicates, an upright delivery begins with the bowler standing erect. Bodyweight is evenly balanced between the two feet and the body is inclined slightly forward

Here are some of the styles of stance plus the names of some of the leading players which use them. STYLE 1 – the Athletic or Upright stance made popular by Willie Wood, who adds a little skip at the end, and Tony Allcock, who adds a wristy flick to his delivery. STYLE 2 – the Low Athletic, popular with Antipodeans John Snell and Peter Belliss; STYLE 3 – the Semi-Fixed, or South African Clinic made popular by Bill Moseley and Doug Watson. STYLE 4 – The fixed made famous by Tom Fleming. STYLE 5 – My England teammates Jimmy Hobday, Dave Crocker and Billy Hobart use this type of extended crouch style.

Stance and delivery

to an extent that is comfortable for the particular individual.

The bowler should be aiming for the optimum mixture of balance and comfort.

The legs and knees should not be stiff but relaxed, remembering to avoid any unbalancing tilt to either side.

The arm holding the bowl may be held slightly to the front and the bowler should take up a position on the mat with feet pointing along the intended line of delivery.

A delivery on the backhand will mean facing to the left (assuming you are right-handed) while forehand shots are taken to the right.

If you are correctly positioned your whole body should be facing along the delivery line, with your trunk at an angle to a line drawn through the centre of the mat to the jack.

The angle will vary with the size of the arc which in turn is governed by the speed of the green.

If you want to make comparisons between the two main delivery positions – the upright and the fixed – it's worth considering the physical logistics of them both.

With the fixed, before the arm starts moving, the left step has been taken. Therefore any subsequent forward weight transfer is limited. And since the knees are already bent the delivery cannot, unless an exaggerated and probably uncontrolled backswing is used, employ the force of gravity to any great extent.

The bulk of required force must come from the arm which is no longer the partly contributory vehicle, but the main spring. The follow through, which is an essential part of any delivery, is therefore very much restricted.

With the upright position both the constant force factors – descent of bowl and forward stride – are involved and are more easily adjustable; so much so that the third factor, muscular contraction, is not used to the same extent.

A constant delivery where the bowl is grounded perfectly every time is essential to every bowler. While no two players appear to have an identical technique, there are certain principles to which the bowler must adhere.

Firstly, from the moment he takes his stance and addresses the green his body must move rhythmically down the aiming line. During the delivery the shoulder, elbow, forearm, wrist and bowl should all stay in line and move along the aiming line with a smooth, flowing action.

The elbow must not be allowed to stray from the side of the body as this will cause a 'hooked' delivery. Neither must the wrist be allowed to twist as the bowl is grounded.

During delivery the bodyweight has to be transferred from the right foot to the left foot and to enable the player to maintain a smooth action I recommend that the left hand is placed on the left thigh to act as a prop. This eliminates or minimises any slight wobble which could result in the player missing his line.

The actual delivery is a combination of a forward step with the left foot and a pendulum-like swing of the right arm.

The bowl is held in front of the body addressing the aiming line and as it swings back and is passing the body, the left foot is raised and moves forward along the line of the delivery. The foot, however, makes contact with the green before the arm has begun its forward swing and it's essential that the knees are bent and relaxed enabling successful transfer of weight to the left foot.

As in most ball games, a smooth follow-through is essential. In bowls this can only be achieved if the bodyweight is well forward over the front foot which dictates that the back foot rises on to the toes or is even raised above the mat according to the power of the swing.

The delivery hand will be pointing along the line, minimising the tendency to hook, jab or flick the bowl, which would make it difficult to control your length.

The bowler must also remember never to lift his head until the bowl has left his hand. It is natural for the body to follow the line and the back foot should be allowed to move forward past the front. It is a good habit to take several steps down the path of the bowl as you regain your upright position.

Whatever stance is used, it is inescapably linked to line and length.

Over the years my own style of delivery has prompted many questions and invariably it is the long backswing with a 180 degree turn of the wrist that bowlers find interesting and they are curious to know if there is any particular value in the exercise.

Delivery must be a relaxed rhythmic action and at no time must there by any tension involved. This applies equally to the arm as to any other part of the body.

When the hand is passing the leg the tension free position is with the palm facing the leg – in other words a 90 degree turn. If we allow our bodies to go limp our hands will automatically drop into this position.

Holding the bowl in the more conventional manner with the palm facing up the green it is only possible to take a normal **backswing in a perfectly straight line** by slightly pivoting the hips as the forward step is taken.

So during delivery the front foot is down the delivery line, as is the shoulder arm and wrist, but the body is angled to the right.

However, with my own style, as the hand makes a complete turn at all times the body remains square to the aiming line. It is only possible to take the arm back in a perfectly straight line by using a full 180 degree turn of the palm.

If one stands with both feet together and takes both arms back simultaneously using the conventional palm-up-the-green technique, one will find that the arms move outwards once they pass the body which emphasises the need to employ the hip pivot when using the popular style. If I adopt the same position with feet together, by a full twist of both wrists I can fully extend my arms behind me, inscribing a perfectly straight line.

This is, of course, due to the construction of the arm and for the same reason it is only possible to clasp ones hands behind ones back by again turning the wrist.

I believe the main advantage of my action is the relaxed position of the arm throughout the delivery and a tension-free arm action must aid better weight control.

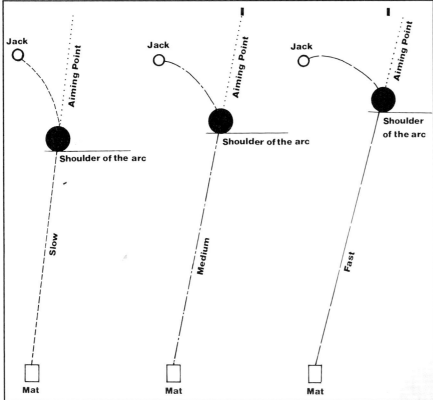

The diagram illustrates the aiming line in relation to the jack on three speeds of green.

It is important to feel the weight of shot you are going to play by 'weighing' the bowl with an up and down motion as you prepare to deliver.

line and of the widest point of the arc the bowl will travel, is very important, and once the imaginary shoulder has been fixed in the mind's eye, the stance should be taken along a line pointing to it. Particular attention should be paid to the placing of the right foot on the mat as it is from this foot that transference of bodyweight takes place during delivery. It is essential therefore that the toe is pointing directly at the imaginary shoulder in the initial stance.

The player must always remember that the 'imaginary shoulder' is not the true shoulder; for if in bowling at the 'imaginary shoulder' his bowl finishes on the jack, his delivery would have passed inside the mark selected. The faster the green the greater effect of the bias, so while on a very slow green the 'imaginary shoulder' and the 'true shoulder' may be relatively close, under very fast conditions they may be several feet apart.

The eyes should never leave this line and every scrap of concentration should be applied to delivering the bowl exactly along it. Even at the moment of delivery and at the end of the follow-through the eyes should be firmly fixed on the 'imaginary shoulder'.

The reason for this is fairly simple. It is far easier to bowl at and hit the mark than to bowl to the arc as a whole. It is easier to bowl *at* something, than *to* something

A left-hander's line will be different to that of a right-hander, but that is because they are bowling on opposite hands – the right-handers' forehand being the left-handers' backhand. As I am right-handed, left-handers will have to swop right for left etc.

Having fixed the line of delivery in your mind you must now determine the weight required to get your bowl to the jack.

Line and length

On the forehand for the right-hander, the bowl is on its way along the aiming line, taken to an imaginary point on the bank . . .

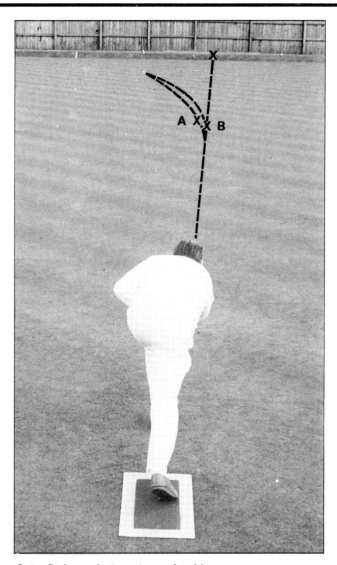

Point B shows the imaginary shoulder, and Point A the position of the bowl on the true should it swing towards the jack.

When I am addressing the green, looking along the point of aim, I 'weigh' my bowl in my hand, moving it up and down to get a correlation with the weight of the bowl and the distance it has to be bowled.

On a faster green you can develop touch with the bowl as it rolls out of the fingers in a nice smooth, flowing delivery. On heavy greens it is more important to grip the bowl because it has to be forced more. It's more difficult to feel length on a heavy green.

To get a really flowing action you need to 'weigh' the bowl – it must come alive in your hands.

It is obviously easier to concentrate and play well on a good green, but you must be prepared to play on greens requiring different weights.

Weight control is undoubtedly the most difficult part of any bowler's game, particularly as the pace of greens can be so variable both home and abroad.

Experienced bowlers from the northern hemisphere do not automatically adapt to the much faster surfaces 'down

under' and vice-versa. It is therefore a skill which is not simple to coach although there are certain basic facts which should always be remembered.

Firstly, good weight comes from the correct propulsion. This is determined by the length of the swing. In this respect it is best to hold the bowl high for a heavy green and use a long backswing and, conversely, keep the bowl low for a fast surface with little or no backswing.

Nevertheless the first consideration must be height of stance as it is impossible to keep a bowl low for a fast green and stand in a vertical position, and it is obviously equally difficult to adopt a bent position and hold the bowl high. In view of this, there is a definite correlation between height of stance and length of backswing which is dictated by the pace of the green, the degrees of which have to be determined by the player according to prevailing conditions. The higher the stance and the longer the backswing, the greater the propulsion. This is not achieved from purely elevation and pendulous action alone, but from the follow through of body weight which plays

On the back hand for the right-hander,
the bowl is again delivered along the
aiming line towards an imaginary point
on the bank . . .

. . . and again the imaginary shoulder
(Point B) is illustrated parallel to the
true shoulder (Point A) as the bowl
continues its curve.

such an important part on the heavier greens of the northern hemisphere. Conversely, on very fast surfaces, like those found in New Zealand, it is crucial that forward body weight should be kept to a minimum. This does not mean that the bowler should keep his trunk in an upright position as it is a vital part of the delivery to lean forward over the bowl in order to achieve the correct follow through, but the majority of weight imparted to his bowl during delivery must come from the arm and wrist. It is therefore imperative that his stance should be as low as possible and that backswing should be restricted to suit the pace of the green.

The heaviest greens of the northern hemisphere and the ultra fast surfaces of the southern hemisphere are extreme conditions but the variations of pace experienced in any one country are considerable and weight control is the most difficult part of the game to master.

The principle of correct elevation and length of backswing to suit the given conditions must be the first consideration and if the bowler is to be a good length player, he must be versatile

and able to vary his stance and backswing yet retain accuracy.

The length of the step will also vary with the propulsion and speed of delivery, but I feel it is best for the player to concentrate on swing rather than step as the latter is invariably sympathetic to the former.

To prove the point, try walking, taking long strides without swinging your arms and try walking taking tiny steps swinging your arms.

I firmly believe that many players confuse themselves by paying too much attention to length of step when bowling under conditions that they find difficult. Their deliveries often become jerky and erratic but had their concentration been placed on length of backswing closely allied to speed of action, the forward step would have been automatically of the correct length and would have been in sympathy with the other two.

Therefore, on heavier greens a longer step and backswing will be needed with a much faster action. If the player's action is copybook, with head down and hand following the line, his back foot will automatically rise above the mat.

Line and length

On fast greens the bowler will take a short step with little backswing and a slow delivery, keeping as low as possible. At the same point of delivery the momentum is such that the back foot should only rise to the toes during follow through.

Every player has a speed of green that suits his own particular style and invariably when he encounters such a surface he immediately settles down and gives of his best. From bowler to bowler this pace will vary to suit the individual's physique and technique. Therefore, it can be said that each player has a natural height of stance, a natural swing, a natural step and a natural speed of delivery.

When encountering conditions ideal to his or her style, a player is almost certainly going to be at peak form. The beauty of the game of bowls is that no two greens are alike and therefore adaptability is the key to success.

Altering the height of stance and increasing or decreasing the length of backswing are the primary considerations and have already been discussed, but the main cause of poor length play which gives the bowler most difficulty is speed of action. It is comparatively easy to adjust height of stance, length of backswing, length of step, etc. but to speed up your action or to slow it down, and still maintain rhythm and flow consistently is far from easy.

This became very apparent to me when I visited New Zealand in 1974 to play in the Commonwealth Games at Christchurch, when I felt that I required more than the ten days allocated for practice to perfect the grooved rhythmic flowing delivery which I would need to combat the surfaces that were sometimes running in excess of 22 seconds.

My return home soon saw me competing in the indoor competitions and playing on our free running indoor carpets which felt to me like bowling on outdoor greens at the beginning of the season.

Naturally, being prepared for the sudden change of pace, I had increased the height of my stance and lengthened my backswing but adjusting the speed of my action again took several weeks to become consistent. I later learned from my fellow members of the England Commonwealth Games team that they had had similar problems.

To summarise, remember length control is governed by three factors: height of stance, length of backswing and length of step. These are governed by the speed of the green and this also determines how firmly the bowl is held. On fast surfaces, it is caressed by the fingers and 'touch play' is the term used to describe successful deliveries.

The pace of the green also determines speed of the delivery action which in turn dictates the amount of forward body-weight required to achieve the correct propulsion yet still retain the smooth, flowing, rhythmic action so necessary to obtain consistent results. While maximum forward body-weigh with a fast delivery action is essential on heavy greens, as the pace of the green increases so both are restricted accordingly. On very fast surfaces forward bodyweight is minimal and a player is encouraged to drop his right knee as he delivers. The speed of the action becomes much slower and more deliberate.

Remember practise makes perfect. Practise your delivery so that it becomes grooved. Every bowl must be grounded the same way. Try bowling at a fixed jack and, keeping the same length, endeavour to draw four bowls close to the jack on line. When you have mastered that, then try it at other lengths. If you can get four bowls to a fixed point every time, you know

that your delivery must be right.

Another excellent test of a grooved delivery is to place a jack approximately in the position of the imaginary shoulder and to bowl directly at it so that your bowl finishes in the centre of the rink. Now if you can reproduce the same delivery action with the next three bowls, all four should finish one on top of the other as they would on the manufacturer's testing table. As the point of aim is determined by the jack, if your delivery is perfect – which means you can hit your point of aim consistently – you only have to repeat the weight of the first bowl with the other three.

It sounds easy but the perfect result is rarely achieved and so much can be learned by the player as to how grooved his action really is.

From your stance first fix your line, then your weight. If a bowler has complete confidence that his mechanics are right, he will be able to bowl under any pressure. A nervous bowler makes mistakes.

Some points to remember . . .

LINE
(1) The 'true shoulder' is always inside the 'imaginary shoulder', and the faster the green the more apparent this is.
(2) Never try to follow a left-hander's line of delivery.
(3) When taking your stance on the mat point the right toe at the aiming point. At the point of delivery the right foot, the elbow, the wrist, the bowl and the aiming point should all be in a straight line.
(4) The eyes must be kept fixed on the point of aim after the bowl has left the hand, that is until the 'follow through' is completed.
(5) Although it is necessary during the stance to keep glancing at the jack to assess weight, when commencing delivery it is imperative that concentration on the point of aim is sufficiently deep to overcome any tendency to look at the jack at the last split second of the action. On a wide hand the jack is usually more or less out of vision, so the temptation is more easily overcome, but the player has to concentrate far more when the draw is narrow and the jack in the periphery of his vision.

LENGTH
(1) Adjust the following to suit the pace of the green: (a) Height of stance. (b) Length of backswing. (c) Forward body-weight. (d) Speed of delivery. (e) Pressure of grip.
(2) Before delivering 'weigh' the bowl in the hand to get a correlation between the weight of the bowl and the distance it has to travel.
(3) Immediately before and during the delivery action (although the eyes are firmly fixed on the point of aim) the player must be concentrating on WEIGHT.
(4) Do not worry about the length of your step. If the height of your stance and length of your backswing are suited to the pace of the green stepping correctly should be automatic.

SLOW GREEN
On slow or heavier greens a long step and backswing are needed with a fast action and upright stance.

MEDIUM GREEN
Less of a forward step and backswing are required for medium-paced British summer greens with a less upright stance.

FAST GREEN
But on the faster indoor surfaces and particularly in Australia and New Zealand only a short step and slow, short backswing are required, keeping as low as possible.

31

The draw shot

The 'bread and butter' shot you must perfect

Bowls players, coaches and anyone connected with the game may argue over many points on the science and techniques of bowls, but there is one point you can guarantee their agreement on – the importance of the DRAW SHOT.

That's not really difficult to understand since the object of the game is to get your bowl as close to the jack as possible.

Although you will in turn learn about all the other shots to store in your armoury, none of them will recompense for any weakness in accurate drawing.

The draw shot is the 'bread and butter' shot of bowls. It's the shot that you have to perfect.

We have discussed how you have to get the correct line and give the correct impetus to place the bowl near the jack. It is

An example of the draw shot   played here on the forehand. The bread and butter shot of bowls, it is the one you have to perfect.

the shot that you will have to practice a great deal and rely on heavily throughout any game.

It is essential that you bowl a good weight and unless you are, in other words drawing well, you cannot expect to be successful with the other shots, which are really variations.

When you play other shots you will have to use slightly different green with a given weight. Unless you know the correct green for the draw, and the correct weight, you cannot play the other shots successfully.

Simply, a draw shot can be described as being a bowl which is delivered up the green in such a way that it comes to rest on or near a particular target. The target in the main will be the jack, but it must be played to any particular spot on the green.

The draw shot has many variations. I am going to deal with just three – the draw, the block and the positional shots.

A draw can be played on either hand, forehand or backhand. We often hear players state that they have a preference for one or the other, but the mechanics for each are identical because if the bowl was perfectly spherical both deliveries would be identical.

However, many bowlers are far more consistent if allowed to play their favourite hand. But assuming their technique is correct the only difference is the shape of the bowl.

In 90 per cent of the instances an irregularity in technique or mechanics is the main cause of an inability to play both sides of the green with confidence. Usually this can be attributed to the whole body not moving down the delivery line, or incorrect positioning of the feet.

If the basic delivery technique is sound with body, arm and feet moving down the line, the discrepancy must surely come from the grip or wrist action. Many players rarely wobble the bowl on their forehands and maintain a fairly consistent line, but when asked to change to the other side of the rink they are far less confident, resulting in a high percentage of erratic deliveries not only in line and length but also the bowler's dread – a wobbled delivery which often invites comments and smiles from other players on the rink.

Although I have given the example of the player who prefers his forehand, there are probably as many who prefer their backhands and are equally as inconsistent when asked to change.

The only obvious difference between the forehand and the backhand shot is the actual grounding position of the bowl. The right-hander playing his forehand will deliver his bowl approximately 12 inches to the right of the matline, whereas on the backhand the grounding will take place approximately in front of the backhand corner of the mat.

The actual grounding position will obviously vary slightly with the pace of the green – the faster the green, the bigger the arc and therefore the player's right foot will have to be angled to the centreline accordingly.

For the left-hander's delivery the reverse will apply – his forehand will be grounded wide of the mat and his backhand in front of the mat, but the positions will be different.

From this we can draw several conclusions. Whereas it is never good policy to try and follow another player's line, it is virtually impossible for a right-hander to follow a left-hander and vice-versa, as the grounding positions of the bowls are approximately 12 inches apart when playing the same hand. Secondly, on a surface where the draw on all four hands is equal, the shoulder of the arc on a player's forehand must theoretically be further from the centreline than the shoulder on his backhand as the bowl is grounded wide of the mat. Therefore a left-hander's point of aim must differ when playing the same side of the rink, always assuming that the bowls are of similar arc, which of course is another variable to be taken into consideration.

So to summarise, too many bowlers are convinced that the backhand and forehand deliveries are as different as 'chalk and cheese' but factually it is all in the mind.

Providing that the feet are correctly positioned on the mat facing the aiming line and the whole body including shoulder, arm, wrist and hand move rhythmically down the line with the bowl held correctly there should be no obvious difference other than the grounding position of the bowl.

There is a subtle difference in as much as the bowl has to be reversed in the hand when changing from forehand to back-hand – that is the large disc always faces the hand that you are playing or conversely the small disc is always innermost. In the past, particularly with lignum vitea bowls which are more spherical, the differing contours of the two sides were far

Right: The difference in line taken by right and left handers is clearly shown here, that's why it is virtually impossible for a right-hander to follow a left-hander's line and vice-versa.

The shorter discs show the average line (at the grounding position) taken on the backhand (left) and the forehand (right), while the taller white discs show the line a left-hander would take – forehand (left) and backhand (right).

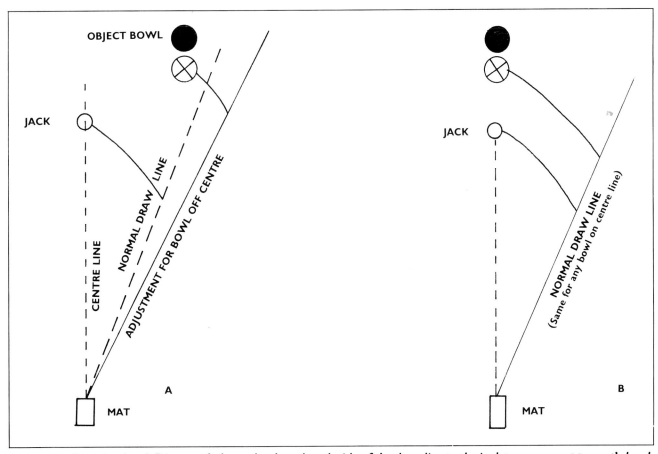

Two types of position bowl. Diagram A shows the shot played wide of the draw line to the jack to cover an opponent's bowl. Diagram B shows a similar shot played with a little extra drawing weight to cover an opponent on the line of the jack.

The draw shot

more easily recognisable but with today's composition bowls, which more than 90 per cent of flat green bowlers use throughout the world, the difference in shape is minimal.

Therefore, if the player ensures that type of bowl is held correctly with the fingers parallel to the running base and the little finger carefully positioned, he should be equally competent on both sides of the rink.

Confidence and concentration help considerably towards sustained accuracy in the draw shot. You must forget what is going on around you and concentrate on your target at the

other end of the green.

If it is a straightforward draw to the jack, particularly if you are the lead or first bowler, convince yourself that the bowl in your hand is going to nestle right on its target.

Don't hurry your shot, take your time and go through the motions I have described above. And if it doesn't come off, forget that one, and concentrate on getting it right next time.

Sometimes it is more prudent to draw up to and against an opponent's 'shot' bowl, especially if that bowl lies within a few inches of the jack, or even to a bowl that may not be shot but

The REST SHOT in action, played drawing weight to rest against an opponent's two bowls and take the shot.

The POSITION SHOT in action. The white discs hold three shots and with his final bowl white positions his shot among his opponent's back bowls as cover against an opposition bid to trail the jack through with his last bowl.

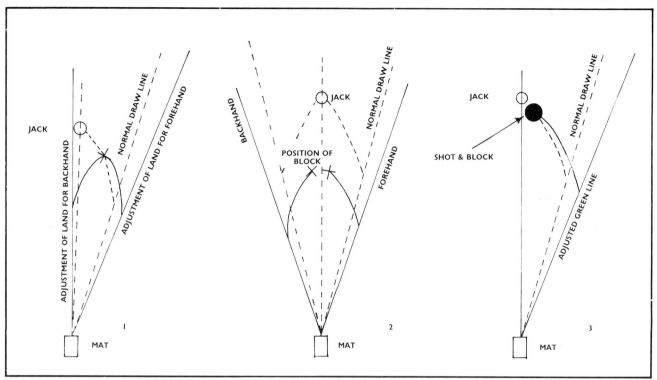

Examples of the BLOCK SHOT . . . played to cover the draw (1), played to cover the drive (2) and played to take the shot and cover the draw (3).

needs to be covered.

This is the POSITION SHOT.

The position shot is basically the draw shot. Again it's just played for a position, which more often than not is behind the jack. It is played exactly the same as the draw shot except that you must allow perhaps a little extra green and weight to get to the position.

Instead of taking the arc back from the jack and playing down the line, you have to take the arc back through the position. Use the marks that you have already established on the green to finish slightly wide of the jack at perhaps a yard behind according to where you, or your skip, wishes you to play.

So you have to re-adjust your mark, the point of aim.

It is a kind of insurance shot to cover an eventuality. If for example your opponents have a number of shots clustered behind the jack, it will be a good idea to get a bowl in with them to nullify the danger if the jack was moved towards them.

If your shot works out, then should the possibility of the jack being moved be turned into fact, you will at least have a chance of cutting down the potential scoring danger, even of getting shot yourself.

When delivering this shot you must concentrate on the exact spot where you want the bowl to finish. This spot is then your target.

A skip must be very definite with his instructions on this shot and indicate the exact spot. It is quite useless just to ask for a 'back bowl'. Obviously accuracy is vital, but despite its importance in the game it is amazing how many bowlers cannot play this shot adequately. Even more amazing is how seldom this shot is practised.

The REST SHOT is purely a draw playing to rest on a bowl.

It may not be possible to draw to the jack because of short bowls. You then make the 'shot' bowl your jack and draw to it, hoping to rest on it.

It is very similar to a positional bowl, the difference being that you are going for a bowl as opposed to a position.

Another type of positional shot is the BLOCK SHOT.

The block shot is a very important bowl but many players avoid playing it because they are frightened that if they do it badly it will be a wasted shot. As its name implies, it is played short of the jack to block the opponent's route to the head.

The object is not only to protect the head but also to force the opponent into attempting the shot that you wish him to play where he may run the risk of giving away more shots. Its value, therefore, if correctly played, is that an opponent has to play a different arc and pace to the one intended.

The best position for the block shot is dependent on many factors.

Every head and every rink is different and this, coupled with the wide variation of arc on greens throughout the world, indicates that rarely are two situations alike. In addition it is important to be able to read your opponent's game – and this assessment of his capabilities will play a large part in determining the exact position of the short bowl.

When playing a block a player has to be quite clear what he is trying to achieve. And unless there are other existing short bowls it is impossible to block your opponent out with one bowl. But if played well short of the head it is invariably more effective, because any bowl making contact with it is less likely to 'wick-in' off, follow-through or punch it into the head.

If played badly it is less likely to act as a guide to an experienced player. It is generally accepted that you block the draw rarely less than four or five feet short of the head,

The draw shot

The BLOCK SHOT in action, in this case delivered well short of the head to protect against an obvious drive or fire by your opponent planning to dislodge those three shots round the jack!

whereas blocking a running or drive bowl in excess of 20 feet short is common practice.

Remember that block shots on a narrow hand are far more effective and far easier to play. On a slow green, where the arc is restricted, a well positioned short bowl will look the size of a football to your opponent.

If he goes outside the bowl he will be struggling to get back and if he plays inside he is likely to be 'narrow'. Conversely the wider the draw and the faster the green, the more difficult it becomes to play an accurate short bowl.

Its value also diminishes as the arc increases as it is in the way. Most players under normal conditions prefer to play overweight shots on the narrower hand, because they expect a higher percentage of success as the margin of error is reduced.

So it can be argued that on fast, wide, drawing greens, block shots are least effective and are mainly used to combat the straight drive. The faster the surface and the bigger the arc the more difficult it becomes to play accurate running shots and every additional second in pace sees a reduction of deliberately short bowls. This is certainly the case on the ultra fast surfaces in New Zealand where the running, bending bowl is seldom if ever played. But it is generally accepted there that if a bowler is to be successful, he must be equally proficient with the draw or the drive.

When attempting the block shot the same principles apply as with drawing to the jack, as it is still the basic draw shot. The point at which the player wishes his bowl to come to rest is the target and the arc should be drawn back from this as for the normal draw.

The target, of course, can be anywhere short of the head and is determined by not only the position of the bowls and jack, but by the type of shot the player is endeavouring to block.

When selecting his line he must remember his pre-determined marks on the bank and green and make the necessary adjustments, bearing in mind that the shoulder of his arc will be three-fifths of the distance from the front edge of the mat to the place he wishes his bowl to finish.

Correct positioning of the feet is therefore essential as good line is more important than good length when playing this type of shot.

When I ask one of my players to play this shot I always say – 'I don't care what you do but get the green right.' When playing a deliberate short bowl a slight variation in weight is acceptable but correct greening is critical as the bowl must finish down the right line.

The other type of block shot is one that is played closer to the head as a shot counter as well as serving to distract your opponent. It will create doubt in his mind and force him to play a shot he doesn't really want to.

But caution is needed, the shot must be played accurately. You do not want to give your opponent an even bigger target.

It is always advisable to play this shot on the true hand as your accuracy will depend on your ability to draw to an imaginary short and off-centre jack.

I don't personally like using a block shot unless everything else is right about the head. But there is no doubt that it pays to use the block shot rather than be greedy and get another shot in the head.

Some critics claim that it can be overcome by a change of position on the mat so as to play inside or outside the block.

A fascinating way to practice the draw shot is by playing target bowls a relatively new innovation, where points are awarded via rings on a rubberised mat. Here the author competes against top crown green star Roy Nicholson in the 1982 British Target championships at Torquay.

This may be so, but the fact that your opponent has to take special steps to overcome the shot clearly shows its value.

There is no substitute for practice in this game. No one, and that applies to me too, ever achieves perfection, but good bowlers develop consistent smooth, fluent and rhythmic deliveries through constant practice.

This is particularly true of the draw shot.

Newcomers coming into the game can practice this shot on their own, providing they can get the green space. I wouldn't at this stage vary the length of the jack; I would stick to the same length, and practice drawing to it until you can get a smooth, rhythmic delivery.

Once you have achieved this then obviously you must change the length. But I am a great believer that if you can find a rhythm on a given length you will be able to keep on repeating it.

Running shots

The shots played with a little extra weight

The DRAW shot will always remain the basic shot in bowls. Success in the game will always depend on its mastery. But the hallmark of the complete bowler is an ability to execute all shots with equal ease.

I divided the types of shots available to the bowls player into three categories and we have looked at the first of these – the draw shot and its variations.

Now we come to those shots played with a little extra weight – the trail, wrest, wick and yard-on.

The TRAIL shot is a slightly faster version of the draw with the object of carrying the jack a short distance. It is one of the most valuable shots in the game, and also one of the most difficult to perfect. Success depends on the ability of a player to take just the right grassline with the exact amount of weight (pace).

The sort of situation where a trail shot becomes necessary could be where your opponent is holding shot, while you have a bowl or two not far behind the jack. It is obvious that moving the jack a short distance back through the head will provide your best opportunity to score.

It must be remembered, however, that your target – the jack – is a much smaller target than a bowl, just 2½ inches approximately in diameter. And you have to hit this target with a bowl that travels on a curved path.

So you can see why line and weight are so important.

In playing this shot, or indeed in asking another player to play it, remember what the objective is and be clear where the bowl is required to finish its course. And remember too that

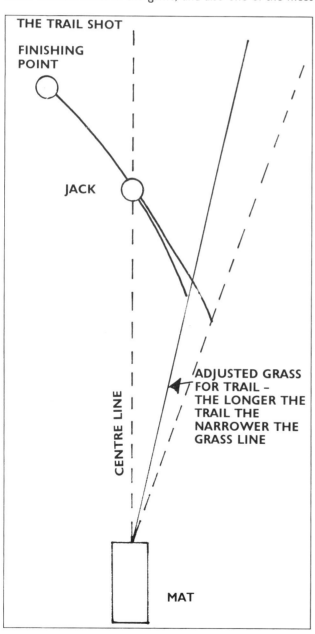

The mechanics of the TRAIL SHOT, showing how the grassline is adjusted depending on the length of trail to be played.

The TRAIL SHOT in action with the white bowl coming in to pick up the jack and trail it to white's back bowls, for three shots.

the jack, when fully struck, will travel approximately the same distance as the delivered bowl – either straight or sideways according to the angle of contact.

With all shots that require just a little extra weight you have to take a narrower line, with the grassline adjusted depending on the length of the trail. Position your feet on the mat accordingly and remember to follow through along the line of delivery to give the bowl sufficient pace.

Another good way of playing this shot is to judge the green that you will have to take and go through your object to a yard or four feet beyond. In other words, you appreciate that if you are going to hit the jack with that given amount of weight, you must be playing a narrow bowl if the bowl was to continue on through the jack.

So many players look at it and say that they will have to cut their green so much. If they bowl that line and if it is the correct line, with the extra weight where will the bowl finish? So they look to the place where they want the bowl to finish and draw a line back through the jack and back to the mat.

That's another way of playing the shot. I have coached players in the past who find this the easiest way to play an overweight bowl.

A successful trail will take the jack from an exposed position to one of safety with a subsequent exchange of shots, and in the case of a full-length head may well result in the jack being taken into the ditch for what might be an unbeatable shot.

There are risks, of course. The jack may be carried too far, or flicked to one side leaving a bad lie, but that is the case with most shots. Usually you wouldn't attempt the shot if there was too much danger, and it is never advisable to play the trail too early in the building of a head.

While the successfully executed trail shot can be a killer, it

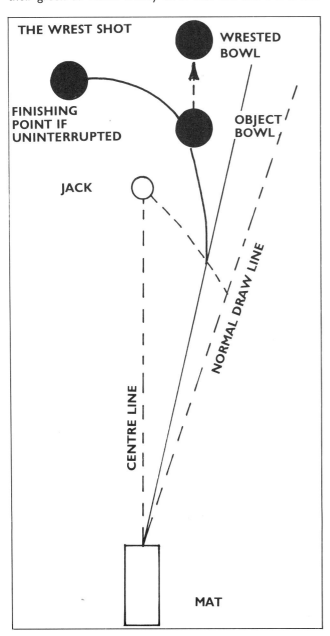

The WREST SHOT is a popular one, the object being to play a bowl out of a favourable position and occupy it with one of your own.

Holding two 'seconds', white comes in to WREST the shot bowl out and replace it with his own for a 'three-count'.

Running shots

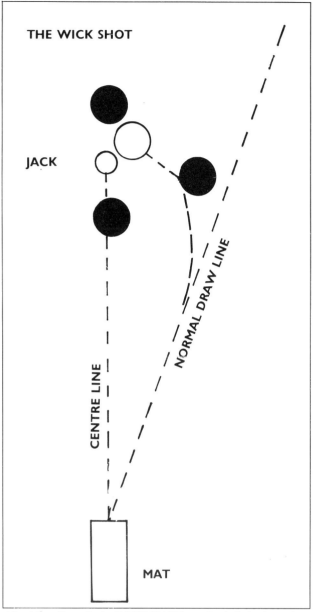

THE WICK SHOT

JACK

NORMAL DRAW LINE

CENTRE LINE

MAT

Much-maligned, the WICK SHOT can look fluky but when played correctly as a legitimate shot can be very effective.

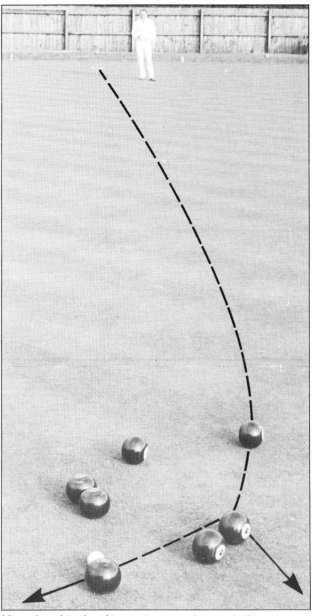

Here the white bowl is coming in with a yard of weight and using one of his own front bowls WICKS in to wrest his opponents shot bowl away from the jack.

must be appreciated that the prevailing conditions should always be taken into consideration before attempting the shot.

The faster the green and the wider the draw, the more difficult the shot becomes. Even if the bowl makes contact with the jack, rarely does it finish in the ideal position. The trail shot is attempted far more often and with a far higher ratio of success on the slower greens and particularly in the northern hemisphere.

This is entirely due to the narrower grass line and the more predictable angle of the bowls entering the head which in turn means that the player can calculate with a higher degree of accuracy the position where the jack is likely to finish.

On faster surfaces the shot is far more difficult with a lower ratio of success and is therefore not attempted as often by the experienced player. The wider arc itself makes the shot more difficult but the main danger is with the bowl's angle of entry

into the head, which is often nearly at right angles.

The player therefore can never be certain whether the jack will be trailed towards the ditch or chipped sideways at right angles which could prove disastrous.

If we take the extreme case of the ultra fast surfaces of New Zealand, the shot is rarely played, as the success rate is so low and more often than not is regarded as 'wasting' bowls.

We talked in the chapter on the draw shots about the variation known as a resting bowl. In this section we look at the WRESTING shot, which differs from the resting bowl because it is played with extra weight – the object being to play a bowl out of a favourable position and to occupy it with your own bowl.

Apart from the draw it is one of the most popular shots in the game.

The principle is the same as the draw except that you are drawing to an imaginary position where your bowl would be

Although the three bowls look to be in good position they should provide few problems to an opposition RUN THROUGH shot to clear the way through.

The RUN THROUGH shot in action as white comes into split the front two bowls away and run on to take the shot.

expected to finish if it was uninterrupted on its course.

To play this shot well requires just the right amount of pace to turn over the shot you want to replace. Your target is the bowl, so you must plot your course back from the bowl estimating the correct line of delivery and the correct shoulder, and back through the bowl to where you want it to finish.

The spot where you, or your skip, wants your bowl to finish is critical because it will determine what pace (weight) you put on the bowl.

Again a good follow through along the line of delivery is essential to help with accuracy.

The ideal wresting shot should theoretically be played with sufficient weight to exactly replace the target bowl – as with a snooker shot. But you would seldom get as smooth a surface as a snooker table in bowls, so you hope that your weight is just correct to achieve its objective.

When skipping I always say to a player who I have asked to play the shot – 'You can wrest that shot out. Imagine your bowl is going to finish on this spot, then that's the weight you require'.

It is also very useful when skipping to indicate that, because it does tend to stop a man playing too heavy and also lets him know that you want a certain amount of weight. This way he doesn't play with too little weight.

Of course, the weight that is played with the shot is governed by the speed of the green. You only have to touch a bowl very gently on a fast green and it goes a long way; but on a slow green you will have to move a bowl quite sharply.

The next in our series of running shots, the WICK is a much-maligned shot. Admittedly it can be fluky on odd occasions, but when played correctly as a legitimate shot it is very effective.

Running shots

On the run . . . the author celebrates a vital shot during the 1980 World Championships in Frankston, Australia, where he took the singles gold medal.

In every end, particularly where bowls are spaced out, it is highly likely that you will get bowls cannoning off each other. Some of these shots may be accidental and it is often difficult to predict the end result. But there are situations where it is possible to draw successfully or to create some other favourable situation by making a deliberate 'wick-off' another bowl.

A fine example of this is when your opponent's bowls are just in front and behind the jack making a direct draw difficult. If there is a side bowl, this can then be used to 'wick-off' to gain the shot by coming on to the jack and in between the two opposing bowls.

The player chooses the bowl that he wishes to play off as his target and concentrates on delivering his bowl so that it makes contact at a pre-determined point on the surface. He has anticipated the line of travel taken by his bowl once it is deflected.

In situations where the grouping of bowls in the head makes other shots impossible, a well executed wick shot can be a match winner. But it's a very difficult shot to play, best exploited outdoors on medium-paced greens. If the surface is slow there may be insufficient rebound; too fast may make the result unpredictable.

Basically the wick can be used to increase the arc of the bowl or to straighten it depending whether the player's bowl makes contact with the target bowl on his bowl's bias or non-bias side.

Bowlers who are experienced snooker and billiard players will readily recognise that this is equivalent to the use of 'running' and 'check' side imparted on the cue ball by the cue.

The actual degree of swing and straightening achieved by the wick is obviously governed by the angle of entry into the head which in turn is determined by the arc and pace of the delivery. A greater variation is possible on a fast green as a bad bowl can enter the head at so many different degrees of wick – three-quarter bowl, half bowl, third bowl, quarter bowl etc – which offers numerous permutations. However, as with most shots in the game, the faster the surface, the more delicate and difficult the shot.

Studying the impact between bowls is a very important part of the game and the experienced player uses the wick *with* the bias and the wick *against* the bias, regularly in all his games.

We often hear a player nominate that he is going to slide in off a bowl, whereas an opponent who didn't hear his nomination might, in passing, refer to it as 'a lucky wick!'

The last shot in group two is the YARD-ON shot.

The so-called yard-on shot is a draw shot played with an extra amount of pace so that your bowl, if its course was uninterrupted, would finish approximately a yard beyond the jack.

You must adjust your feet on the mat to take a narrower line of delivery than the draw, and give the bowl enough force to come to rest not more than a yard beyond the jack.

Too many players, when asked to play this shot, get the weight all wrong and finish up by putting on several yards of pace, going well beyond the position that the bowl was intended, although it must be remembered that this shot is usually played as an attacking bowl.

A yard-on shot is usually called for when it is necessary to disturb bowls in the head. You are playing what I would describe as an attack and lie shot, playing to come in and disturb the head, hoping to move shots and make the position better.

The other reason is to place a bowl in position at the back of the head, usually asked for in a game of fours by the skip or his No.3, as an insurance shot.

Control of the yard-on shot is not easy and in certain conditions I don't think it should be attempted. Slow to medium-paced greens, that is those of 12 to 14 seconds, are the most suitable but on a faster green a player should be most cautious as in these conditions it is the hardest shot in the game to control.

On a fast green the size of the target should have a large bearing on your decision about playing the shot. If the target is two or three bowls together then your chances of wresting them are good, but if you are confronted with just trailing the jack back a yard, think hard about it.

It is also easier to play on short ends than on long ones. Despite all this it is necessary for any aspiring player to master this shot, although the 'yard-on' term has been abused by many skips, coming to mean any shot played into the head with force. It should mean a shot that is one yard over the draw.

Some points to remember . . .

THE TRAIL
(1) It is a very difficult shot but can be played with a fair degree of success on greens of 13 seconds or less. On greens of 14 seconds plus, due to the wide arc, even if the player makes contact, the jack rarely ends up in the right place.
(2) When attempting the shot draw an arc through the jack to the finishing position and bowl down the line. But remember the 'true shoulder' is inside the 'imaginary shoulder'.

THE WREST
(1) This is a similar shot to the trail but as the object is a bowl and not the jack a much higher degree of success can be expected since the target is much bigger.
(2) It is attempted in a similar manner to the trail but weight varies slightly according to how far the bowl has to be displaced.

THE WICK
(1) While the wick is often a lucky shot, when players of a high standard are competing the shot is played more often than not.
(2) Study the impact between bowls – be conversant with plants or sets and recognise how to slide off the bowls to increase the angle of entry into the head and how to make contact to check and straighten the path of the bowl.
(3) Wick shots are normally played with a yard or two yards of running but there are occasions when a player has to fire to wick off a bowl when he is several shots down and the direct path to the jack is hopelessly bocked.

THE YARD ON
(1) Like the trail, the yard on shot is easier to play on slow and medium paced greens. The faster the surface the wider the draw and the more critical weight control becomes.
(2) The yard on shot is usually played as a percentage shot where there are several chances – that is if you miss the object there is always a chance of doing something else, like wresting a bowl or trailing the jack.

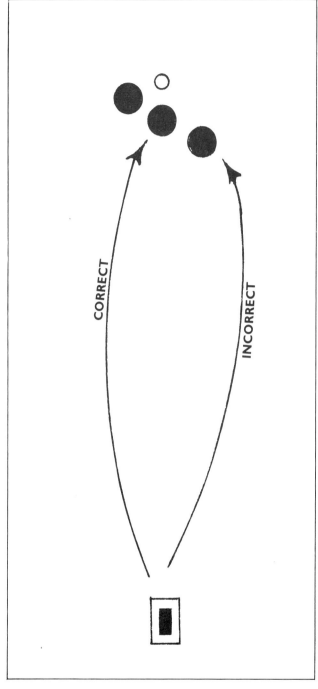

The opposition bowls are placed a little awkwardly, but a back hand shot (for a right-hander) played as a run through, presents the best opportunity here.

(3) Do not forget that success with all running shots stems from bowling good length. Unless you really know the pace of the green for drawing shot the more difficult combination of a new weight and a new line could prove disastrous (and often does) if attempted too early in the game.

Heavy shots

The run-through, the heavy bowl and drive

Flat Green bowls is a game of tactics. It is a case of playing a variety of shots to score, and also trying to prevent your opponent(s) from doing the same.

The draw shot is the basis from which your play will be built-up but there will also be occasions where you will need to either retrieve a situation where shots are against you, or alternatively remove a bowl in order to gain a count or add to an existing count.

This is where the heavy shots come into play. It is not always easy to distinguish what is termed a firm shot, a firm bowl which cannons off another to achieve its objective or a firing shot – but they all have their tactical uses.

A lot depends on the pace of the green. On a slow paced green it may be necessary to play only a firm shot, whereas on a fast green a full-blooded firing shot would be required.

In general, firm shots are mainly attempted on slow to medium paced greens similar to those found in the UK, where a high degree of success can be achieved. They are usually played where a situation has built up that leaves little alternative.

While I agree that the first intention of any head is to draw successfully, if that situation hasn't occurred then there comes a moment when a rescue attempt must be mounted. Quite clearly a firm or firing shot into a cluster of bowls is the only way in which to cause a change round in fortunes.

So when the strategy calls for you to attack, it's then a case of deciding just how much weight is required to achieve your objective. The first shot to consider is the FOLLOW THROUGH or RUN THROUGH shot.

The objective of this shot is to play on to the short bowls of a closed head with sufficient pace to 'follow' or 'run through' into a scoring or saving position. It is a particularly valuable shot on heavy or holding greens when short bowls often block the head. A lot depends on how far you wish your bowl to run through in determining the amount of pace (weight) required, with the necessary reduction in grassline.

A skip should therefore clearly indicate where he requires the bowl to finish, if its course is uninterrupted, thus giving an indication of the pace required. If the bowl is required to run through the head about a yard, several yards of extra pace with the necessary narrower grassline will be needed, but both will vary as they are dependent on the pace of the green.

The shot should never be played if, by moving the jack with the object bowl, a loss of shots could result.

A variation of this shot is where there are two bowls obscuring the jack and a run through shot will split them and leave either a clearer view or take shots. The shot is basically to take out the bowls as opposed to moving the jack, but it can be played to finish with a jack trailing situation.

The HEAVY BOWL shot is played with at least ditch weight, which means that if you miss your object and make no contact with any other bowls in the head, then you would lose your bowl.

It is not a full-blooded drive because, depending on the pace of the green, your bowl will arc for a few feet. On a very fast green with little grip, one can expect a big draw, but when you play with weight, the arc is greatly reduced, varying, of course, with the degree of weight used. So on a fast green, say of about 16 seconds, where the friction of the playing surface is minimal it is possible for most bowlers to drive or fire straight at their objective.

On an average paced green the bowl makes 75 to 80 per cent of its arc during the last 20 to per cent of its journey, in

Driving my way

Heavy shots

other words, as it loses momentum the bias action increases. The bowler has to remember when playing a running bowl that if he increases his weight by 20 to 30 per cent he must expect to reduce his green by at least two-thirds. This is particularly evident and particularly difficult to gauge on the hard, fast surfaces of the southern hemisphere.

It must also be understood that on very heavy greens, where the initial propulsion is excessive, the bowl will appear to run almost straight to the shoulder of the arc whereas on fast surfaces the bias action comes into effect from the point of delivery as it is rolling at a far greater pace.

On a slower green it is more difficult to drive straight because the friction pulls your bowl up more quickly tending to send the bowl arcing across the front of the head.

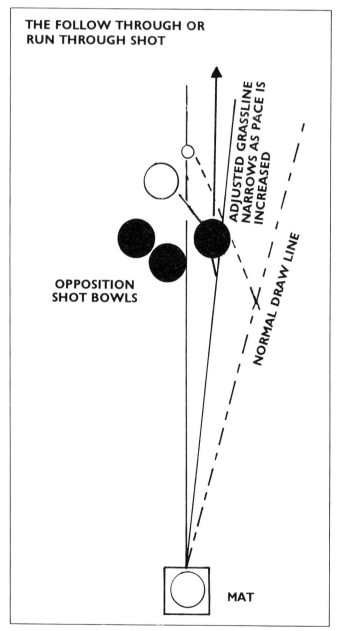

THE FOLLOW THROUGH OR RUN THROUGH SHOT

ADJUSTED GRASSLINE NARROWS AS PACE IS INCREASED

NORMAL DRAW LINE

OPPOSITION SHOT BOWLS

MAT

The follow through or run-though shot . . . my bowl (white) is played firmly to force the right-hand (black) bowl through the head and follow through to take shot.

However, the same principle applies, as on any surface the bias action of the bowl is at its greatest during the last quarter of its journey. The difference in arc when playing the running bowl is not so evident on a slow green as the draw is nowhere near as great, but the player still has to reduce his green in accordance with the extra weight he imparts.

In view of this it is not surprising that the running bowl is used mostly on the holding surfaces where the variety in arc is more easily calculated and where a slight discrepancy in weight is not so heavily penalised.

This shot is most valuable when it is necessary to take a bowl off or out of the head, to take a jack through to the ditch and also when it is necessary to bend round short bowls.

A player should not fix his eyes on the objective but, as with the draw shot, look along the grassline. The arm and feet should normally follow the direction of the eyes as there could be a marked tendency to play this shot narrow if looking at the object.

As with most of the running shots it is a percentage shot which should only be played when the chances of success are favourable and failure will not leave you vulnerable to a loss of shots.

A fast shot with just a little allowance for bias is called a FIRM shot.

There is a diversity of opinion regarding the merits of the firm shot as opposed to a drive. But they are two different shots, used for different purposes.

The firm shot is a controlled shot, delivered at varying speeds to promote bowls, take a bowl out and even ditch the jack. It is also used in preference to the drive on heavy or wet greens or when lack of physical strength prevents a drive. On heavy greens a firm shot can gain many shots, whereas on faster greens where there are more gaps for bowls to pass through the firm shot is not as easy as the drive to play.

The ability to play both shots is essential for all experienced bowlers and the individual will have to use his own judgement as to which to employ when required.

Very often a position will occur during a game in which the removal of a bowl for extra shots is impossible with a drive because bowls are lying in direct line of the objective. So a firm shot is the one to play.

In delivering the firm shot, the amount of green you will take will depend entirely on the pace of the green. Position your feet to take a narrower line of delivery. Because you are using a shot with weight you will take a slightly longer step forward, which will also increase your backswing, enabling you to get the required force behind the shot.

A good follow-up along the line of delivery is very important.

It is a shot that requires a great deal of care and accuracy because it is always difficult to gauge the grassline in relation to the amount of pace.

We now come to what many bowlers would term the last shot in the bowlers armoury, the DRIVE or FIRING shot.

Many bowlers regard this as the most controversial shot in the game, and it has certainly been the subject of frequent arguments and discussions. But this shot has become more popular and practised more frequently in the modern game, and I firmly believe that anyone who aspires to become proficient in this game must be able to play it.

There are a number of occasions when the drive becomes a necessity.

The need to pick out a single bowl or bowls which is, or are, in view, to break-up the head in order to cut out shots and give room for a more advantageous shot; the need to take the jack out of the confines of the rink to give a dead end and therefore a completely fresh start; or to drive the jack into the ditch for a count.

The drive shot is delivered on the green so that the bowl runs in almost a straight line, which means it must have enough force to counteract the inbuilt bias of the bowl.

To play the shot most effectively you will need to adopt an athletic stance, sighting your bowl almost to or at chin level. This is why it is always so obvious when I am going to play this shot.

The grip I favour for this shot is the claw. But I see no reason why the cradle cannot be equally as effective provided the technique is perfect. The most important factor is that the bowl should be forced firmly into the palm and firmly gripped. As there is no touch required in the drive shot, the player can dispense with finger control. The sheer speed of the movement ensures that the bowl is released at the right time if the delivery technique is sound.

The same precautions should be taken with the grip for the drive as for any other shot. That is, the fingers should be parallel to the running base of the bowl and it should feel comfortable in the hand.

Don't try to 'wobble' a bowl by turning it slightly over in the

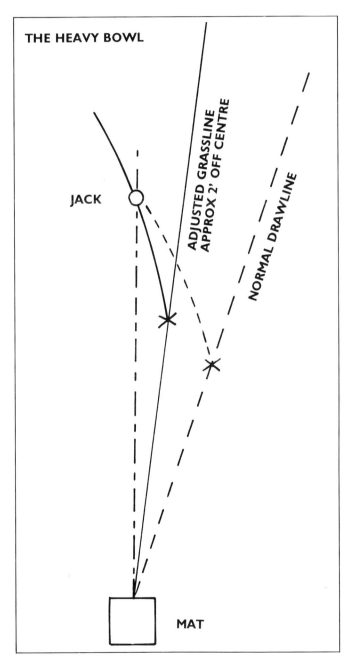

The heavy bowl. . . the diagram shows how the grassline is reduced to take the jack through. A general principle for a 30 per-cent increase in pace is an arc reduced by two-thirds.

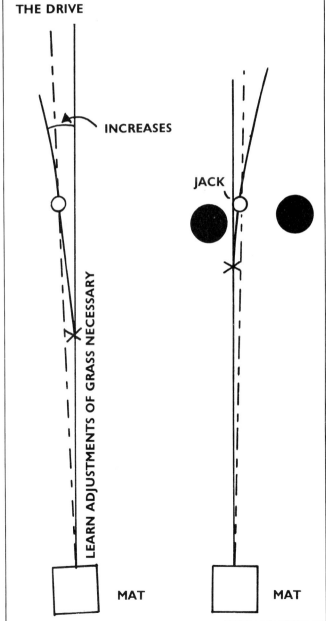

This shot is usually delivered with enough force to almost completely counter the in-built bias of the bowl. The bowl needs very little grassline and on the fast greens of Australia and New Zealand, probably none at all.

Heavy shots

grip to make it hold-up more for a drive. Players who find that their bowls are biasing away from the head before it reaches the objective should increase the amount of green instead, and keep the bowl on an even keel.

The movement is the same as for the draw shot except that the backswing for the drive is naturally longer, which increases the length of both forward swing and step.

As the delivery swing is much faster it is essential to get a smooth action. The tendency when you speed things up is that something is more likely to go wrong. The backswing can be slowed slightly and the pace increased when the bodyweight is transferred forward. There is a distinct danger that if the backward movement isn't smooth, it will throw you off line.

The bodyweight is well forward when driving.

During your delivery do not allow your eyes to leave the course you have selected. Allow the back foot to follow through after you have released the bowl and do not lift your head until the bowl is well on its way.

When you deliver a driving shot you are putting so much momentum behind your bowl that your whole body will want to follow through. Don't be afraid to come off the mat after the bowl has been released – two or three strides down the green. It is essential to get a good follow through.

Learn to drive on both hands. Some players tend to use one hand just for firing. Fred Horn, an English international from 1949-65, was held in high esteem because of his uncanny accuracy with the drive. But it was only in recent years that it was pointed out to me by another Devon international that he always fired off the same hand. I personally had a preference for playing this shot purely on the backhand. Now I don't mind.

It is better to be able to drive on both hands, although some players prefer the forehand because they say the arm swings outside the body, allowing a straight follow through. However, if the mechanics are right in theory there is no difference.

What you have to remember is the grounding of the bowl. With the forehand it will be slightly inside the edge of the mat, while with the backhand in the middle of the mat.

As mentioned before, driving is easier on fast greens as the bowl maintains its delivery speed longer, preventing it from turning. The same can be said for short and long jacks on a heavy green. You may be able to drive straight on a short end but a long jack will require either more speed or green.

If a player finds that when he attempts to drive fast he can't control direction and loses his touch for the draw shot afterwards, then it would pay him to reduce the speed and allow a little more green. Alternatively he could adopt a different stance for the drive, particularly if he bowls from the crouch or semi-crouch position.

Never sacrifice direction for speed.

In the firing line

A straight drive when used with skill and discretion is probably one of the most effective shots in the game of bowls and is invaluable as a measure of defence. And if brute force works then it's justified.

In singles it is sometimes the only ploy when you are playing an opponent who is drawing to the jack better than yourself. However, beginners are advised to forget driving until many, many months of practising the draw shot.

In my experience as a bowler I have never known a top class player who has relied solely on the draw shot. Those who succeed at this game have a full armoury of shots. What is important is to perfect all shots which requires constant practice.

Points to remember

THE FOLLOW THROUGH OR RUN THROUGH SHOT
(1) Particularly valuable on a rink with narrow draws.
(2) Very effective on a holding green with tight heads.
(3) To be used with discretion on swinging and difficult hands.

THE HEAVY BOWL
(1) Usually played with at least ditch weight but still allowing the bowl to swing.
(2) More effective on wide drawing head as a shot played with less weight is infinitely more difficult.
(3) A valuable shot for taking a bowl out or running the jack into the ditch. Most often played when weight is not critical but allowing the bowl to bed is essential.

THE FIRM SHOT
(1) This is generally the alternative to the straight drive. Sometimes a player feels happier allowing his bowl to bias slightly as he is satisfied that he is less likely to dislodge his own bowls than with a straight drive.
(2) It is often used on wet slippery surfaces as the chances of a bowl skidding are greatly reduced.
(3) Sometimes this is the only method of taking out a bowl hidden in the head. The slight biassing of the bowl achieves the object whereas the straight drive would be futile.

THE DRIVE OR FIRING SHOT
(1) A shot to be practised until the player knows his margin of error. He has to be consistently close to his objective and be confident that under pressure he will not produce a wild one and do more damage than good.
(2) Indiscriminate firing loses matches equally as much as quality firing wins matches.
(3) Concentrate on perfecting weight transfer at speed. This is far more difficult than doing it at a comfortable pace.
(4) While a different stance for firing is not essential it is to be recommended as most bowlers find it difficult to draw after they have played several heavy shots.
(5) This is the one shot where the bodyweight can be put well forward and the bowl really gripped tightly. The player should be aware that the body feels that it wants to fall down the line. This helps weight transfer and also produces more pace.

Physical fitness

To most non-bowlers our game appears one of gentle tranquility played on balmy, sunny afternoons with the cares of the world all forgotten.

It's an image that has persisted for some time coupled with the feeling that you don't need to be very fit to play bowls.

But bowls, particularly nowadays, just cannot be dismissed lightly as a game for physical geriatrics, although many who have a physical handicap can fortunately enjoy the game.

Performance in any sport depends firstly on a grasp of the basic techniques coupled with the bodily fitness to carry it out. Tired muscles will invariably lead to faults in technique and in some cases physical damage.

While it cannot be contended that bowls is a tremendously strenuous game requiring rapid movement, it does nevertheless involve the use of muscular movement which will be considerably helped if the body is kept strong and supple.

If you start your bowling career early in life you will develop, hopefully, a smooth, rhythmic delivery. But you may not be able to maintain this as you get older. I have emphasised the importance of absolute leg-control in my style of delivery and although I have found the most comfortable action, I need to ensure that my body is kept fit and supple.

It must be remembered that a game of bowls, particularly at competitive level, does take some time and there is no doubt that unfit muscles must tire by the end of the game. With tiredness comes the development of faults – loss of balance, inaccurate gripping and grounding of the bowl and jerky delivery.

Also, physical tiredness does not come alone. It invariably leads to a lethargic approach with a steady decline of the powers of concentration so vital if a player is to maintain a high standard of play.

So while it is still possible for a bowler to perform for just about as long as he can stand-up, the fitter bowler will find that he can enjoy his sport and perform that much better.

There are two areas on which to concentrate – weight control and keeping the legs, spine and arms in a supple condition. As a bowler will spend most of his time on his feet, and will use his hands frequently as well, these should not be ignored.

It is important for me to keep my weight under control, because any unnecessary weight could affect my delivery and possibly on a day involving several matches cause excess tiredness. So I cut down on bread, potatoes, sugar and allied products. There is no need to get out the calorie-control charts, being aware and just careful will go a long way.

Everyone who knows me also knows that I am partial to a drink of beer, but I never have more than a shandy between matches. On a very hot day it will tend to dull the senses a bit, so leave the beer until after the match.

Now those exercises . . .

Bowling is in itself a perfect form of exercise. Properly played there is little physical strain, particularly to heart and lungs. But it has been estimated that for a game of pairs of 21 ends you will get three hours of rhythmic arm and body exercise, walk about a mile, bend over at least 160 times and lift approximately 300lbs of bowls and propel them two miles.

During some tournaments a player could be on the green for up to 15 hours!

About 12 years ago I developed some problems with my back and to counteract these I turned to the ancient Eastern art of Yoga. I have found that by doing a series of exercises for about three-quarters of an hour each day I can keep my body supple.

Yoga for me looks after my spine, arms and legs.

But I must stress that these exercises should not be attempted without proper instructions because if not done properly injury could be caused. Be fully aware of the benefits – but aware of the dangers.

The exercises I undertake come in the **ASANA** class. Asana is the Sanskrit word for posture and occupies third place in the steps of traditional Yoga.

The first is the **HALASANA** or The Plow as it is known.

This pose is one of the most powerful of the asanas and treats simultaneously the entire spine, heart, lungs and nerves. It should be done very slowly and on an empty stomach. The tension from this pose is on the outside of the spine, compression inside. It will also help to reduce excess fat around the waist and hips.

AIMS
1. To invert the trunk and stretch the spine, stimulate the nerves and tone all organs and glands.

PROCEDURE
1. Lay on your back with legs apart.
2. Breath in, raise legs at right angle to body.
3. Breathe out and upon breathing in . . .
4. Roll feet in an arc over the head.
5. Keeping legs straight, place feet as close to head as possible.
6. Stretch arms over head.
7. Breathe **in** and **out** slowly.
8. Slowly move feet away from head.
9. When maximum stretch is achieved, place hands forward again, reverse order.
10. Relax supine (face up).

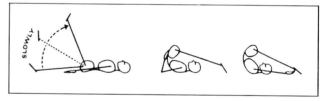

POINTS TO WATCH
1. Don't be too hasty.
2. Not enough muscle control which will cause a sudden jerk in position four.
3. Don't bend your knees.
4. Don't jerk your head off floor on return.
5. Don't breathe too deep or too fast.

PASCHIMOTASANA (The back stretching position).
Of all the Yoga poses the Paschimotasana is one of the most effective for improving and maintaining health. It is specially recommended as a preparation for practising meditation.

In the beginning the complete asana may be held from three-five seconds. With practice this can be extended to one minute.

It is a great aid to strengthening abdominal muscles.

AIMS
1. To stretch tendons, muscles and vertebrae of the lower legs and spine.
2. To massage the heart, increase peristalic (digestion) action and to tone-up the entire body.

3. To induce beneficial intra-abdominal compression.
4. To stretch and tone the sciatic nerve.

PROCEDURE

1. Sit with legs straight out.
2. Hands on thighs.
3. Hang head forward.
4. Breathe out, lean forward as far as possible extending hands to feet.
5. Resume first pose. Repeat series three to six times (this procedure is to prepare and relax back and posteria muscles).
6. Grasp toes with fingers and pull head to the knees and elbows to the floor.
7. Relax supine (face up).

POINTS TO WATCH

1. Legs bending is most common. Try to keep back to knees on the floor, but take care.
2. Strain on the back and posteria muscles, make sure that they get a preliminary stretch.
3. Not removing the tension on the stomach muscles once feet have been grasped.
4. This pose isn't always advised for younger women as it increases in abdominal pressure.

The **MAHA MUDRA** is a variation of the Pachimotasana.

When in the preparatory posture for the Pachimotasana, place the heel hard into the perenium, sole against the thigh, then proceed as advised for the Paschimotasana. Alternate with other leg. This may be done with the foot above the thigh, as in the lotus position.

These asanas are very difficult at first, as the back muscles will not stretch to allow the full forward movement.

When opposition from these muscles is relaxed away, the pose is 95-per-cent achieved.

DHANURASANA (The Bow).

This simple exercise is excellent for improving the elasticity of the spine. All the spinal nerves are toned, generally increasing the efficiency of the body. It is useful because the backward curve pulls the posterior prominences of the vertebra together, while stretching the anterior part. The lumbar and abdominal muscles are given a most beneficial stretch and it reduces adipose tissue around the waist, buttocks and stomach.

AIMS

1. To constrict muscles over back surface of the body.
2. To stretch those of the front.
3. To induce maximum curvature of the vertebra.
4. To tone entire nervous system.

PROCEDURE

1. Exhale.
2. Grasp ankles.
3. Pull on legs as on a bow.
4. Curve head back, chin up.
5. Hold for about twelve counts.
6. Break slowly, and relax for twelve counts.
7. Repeat for up to four times.
8. Relax supine (face up).

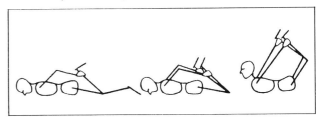

POINTS TO WATCH

1. Knees swinging apart.
2. Tendency to pull arms with toes instead of vice versa.
3. Not stretching neck and back in proper position.
4. Not lifting knees at all, placing all the stretch on the torso.

BUJANGASANA (The Cobra)

The spinal column is a marvellous system of tendons, muscles, ligaments and tissues which gives the spine both incredible strength and maximum movement. This pose gives benefits to the whole system by exercising all the vertebrae from the first cervical to the last lumbar.

The blood supply to the spine depends on the general muscle tone of the system for its efficient circulation. The posture rejuvenates the spinal muscles and as a result of stretching, the abdomen also receives help. The heart benefits from alternative increase and decrease of pressure. However, people with over active thyroid glands or weak kidneys should NOT perform these poses.

AIMS

1. To stretch and compress in the same manner as the Bow.
2. To exercise the vertebrae one after the other.
3. To develop spinal muscles, control and strengthen and to tone up kidneys, thyroid and adrenals.

PROCEDURE

1. Lay face down, forehead on floor.
2. Place palms on floor close to shoulder.
3. Move head so that chin comes on to the floor.
4. Move as far forward as possible.
5. Breathe out and curve trunk back vertebra after vertebra until tension reaches lumbar.
6. Push down on hands.
7. Stretch up like a snake bringing head forward.
8. Hold for a count of 12.
9. Uncoil in reverse order breathing out.

rhysical fitn ss

POINTS TO WATCH

1. Not concentrating on cervical curve.
2. Letting the head come forward first on the uncoil.
3. Placing too much weight on the hands instead of letting the back muscles take the weight.

Like the bow it can be held for sometime while breathing when proficient, but take care not to strain the sacro-illiac.

ARDHA VAJRASANA (Reclining Adament Pose)

The Vajrasanas are a series of postures which help to correct faults in posture, aid digestion and tone up the limbs. They also stretch the ankles.

AIMS

1. To stretch tissues in the thighs.
2. Curve the vertebra.
3. Tone muscles, tissues and nerves in the pelvic cavity.
4. Stretch muscle tissue in the chest and shoulder.
5. Tone up lungs.

PROCEDURE

1. Sit in kneeling position.
2. Toes touching, sit between heels.
3. Hands on knees, spine straight.
4. Leaning back place right elbow on floor.
5. Repeat with left.
6. Curve spine and lower crown of head onto floor.
7. Stretch arms over head.
8. Relax breathing, deep slow and rhythmic.

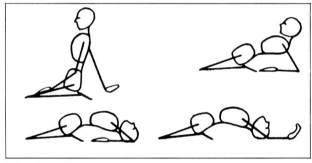

POINTS TO WATCH

1. Knees lifting off floor.
2. Knees spreading apart.
3. Strain on the thighs.
4. Ankles will not stretch sufficiently.
5. Too great a strain on the sacro-illiac.

Tension can be alternated between thighs and the sacro-illiac by alternatively allowing the knees to lift and separate and then bringing them together again during retention of the pose. Time limited to three minutes. Improper and hasty practice can cause lesion on the sacro-illiac.

There are two further variations of this pose. One by further stretching and letting the back of the neck onto the floor and by lowering the head to the floor without the assistance of the hands and elbows. The last should only be attempted after cautious experiment.

CHAKRASANA (The Wheel)

There are a group of poses which includes the chakrasana whose effects, although slightly different, all have the maximum effect on the elasticity of the spine.

The use of all these complimentary poses assures the complete and all round exercise of this most important area of the body.

A few turns of the chakrasana is extremely exhilarating giving the arms and legs balanced training while toning up the front tissues of the torso, but do NOT attempt on slippery floors or mats.

The pose can also be assumed from the standing position. If attempting it from the erect position a wall can be used as a support. The breath should be held in while making a backward curve, feet well apart with knees inclined together and weight on the inner edge of the feet. Hold for five seconds at first, increase to 15 seconds maximum.

AIMS

1. To exercise the entire spine, its ligature, muscles, nerves and blood supply.
2. To stretch muscles and tissues of the body's front surface.
3. To compress muscles and tissues of the body's posteria area.
4. To tone up the endrocrine system, particularly the thyroid and adrenals.
5. Strengthen muscles and walls of the abdomen.
6. Increase body heat and energy.

METHOD

1. Can be achieved from the standing bent back position, or from a position on the floor.
2. Knees bent, feet on floor, 12 inches apart.
3. Palms on ground next to ears.
4. Breathe in, press up into pose.
5. Breathe slowly and carefully hold.

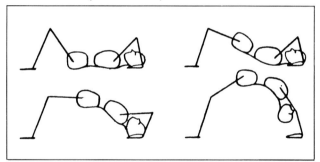

POINTS TO WATCH

1. Strain on the wrists. They may have to be trained by elevation poses first.
2. Getting up on toes.
3. Separating the legs too much.
4. Holding for too long. Relax if you begin to tremble.
5. Feet or hands slipping if done on slippy surfaces.

People with blood pressure or hernia should be very careful – but the pose can be beneficial. Hold for 5-15 seconds maximum.

A regular exercise programme will help the bowler. Healthy muscular fatigue encourages normal sleep and rest. And healthy physical exercise can help towards preventing hardening of the arteries.

There are also the implications towards mental health, but that will be dealt with in the psychology of bowls.

● Drawings and assistance in compilation of this chapter have been provided courtesy of Transworld Publishing, of Cavendish House, London, Publishers of the Corgi pocket-book of YOGA by Russell Atkinson.

Physical fitness

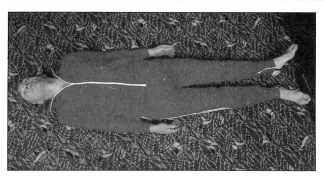

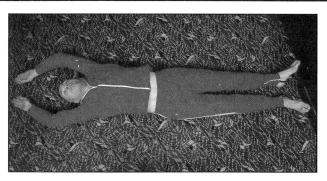

THE PLOW

Halsana, or The Plow, treats spine, heart, lungs and nerves. David starts by lying flat on his back.

The whole exercise should be done very slowly. David now extends his arms beyond the head and breathes in. Do not breathe too deep or too fast.

MAHA MUDRA

Maha Mudra is a variation of Paschimotasana commencing in an upright sitting position.

Bring one heel into the thigh, hang head forward, breathe out and stretch as far as possible to the extended foot. It will take time to achieve full movement.

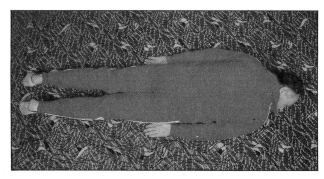

THE COBRA

Bujangasana, or The Cobra, benefits the entire spinal column. Begin by lying face downward, forehead on floor.

Place palms on the floor close to your shoulders, move head so that the chin comes on to the floor and moves as far forward as possible.

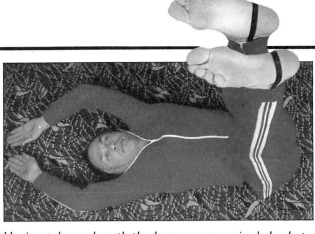

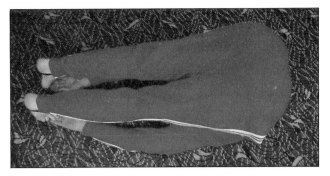

Having taken a breath the legs are now raised slowly to right angles, keeping the knees straight. Breathe out.

On the next breath the feet are brought down in an arc over the head. Breathe in and out slowly before returning to the start position and relax.

Breathe out and curve the trunk backwards vertebra after vertebra until tension reaches the lumbar. It is important to concentrate on the cervical curve.

Push down on hands and stretch up like a snake, bringing head forward. The pose is normally held for a count of 12 before uncoiling in reverse order.

Physical fitness

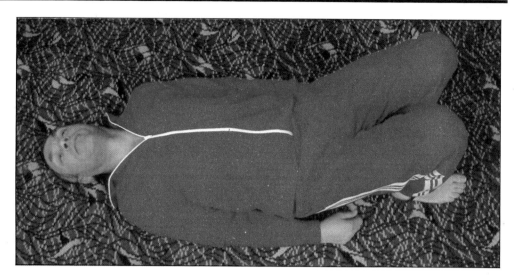

THE WHEEL

An exhilarating exercise is Chakrasana, or The Wheel, which apart from assisting the spine also trains arms and legs and tones up front tissues of the torso. Begin by lying on the floor, knees bent and feet about 12 inches apart. Next place your palms on floor by the ears and, breathing in, press up into pose. Hold for 5-15 seconds maximum and beware of strain on wrists or sliding on slippery surfaces.

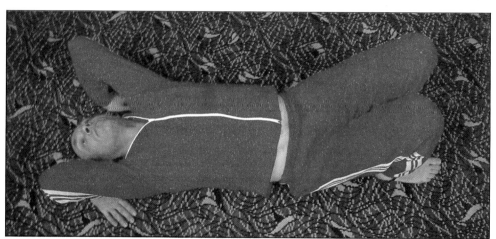

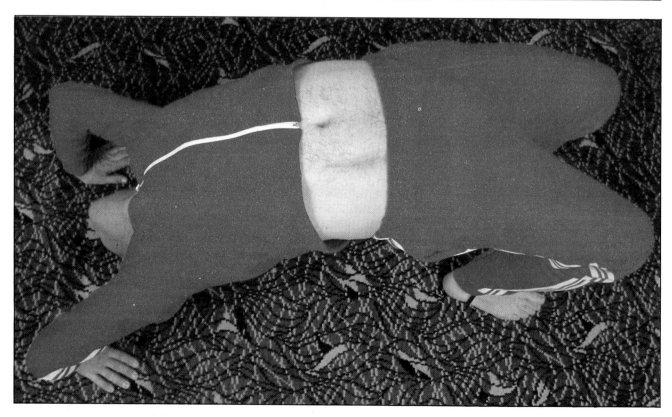

CONCENTRATION

Study of the green

Skill of reading indoor and outdoor surfaces

Bowls, both indoor and outdoor, is played on a variety of surfaces which all have their own peculiarities in terms of resistance, consistency and in the case of outdoor greens, surroundings.

So being able to read your green is an important skill to acquire.

Let's deal with outdoor surfaces first.

The texture of greens can vary greatly. Grass greens can be well-cut or long, the ground can be hard or soft and bumpy or smooth. The net effect of all these factors is that the bowl will take differing times to reach the jack and you may need to make adjustments in the amount of land you take to counteract the conditions.

One of the first things to explain is the peculiarity regarding the speed of a green.

In bowls terms when we talk about the green being fast it means that the bowl starts at a slower pace and will take longer to reach the jack. Alternatively, on a slow green the bowl will start at a faster pace and reach the jack sooner.

So if you convert that to seconds, when you hear someone say that 'the green is slow', then they mean around 10 seconds. Anything upwards of 14 seconds would be fast.

And to put that completely into perspective, the time figure quoted is the length of time it would take a bowl to travel from the moment of delivery to stop at a jack at 30 yards away.

Now at first this might sound a little technical but broken down to basics you will see why it is important to know the pace of the green you are bowling on.

On the slower greens the path of a draw shot will be more direct therefore you will have to take a narrower line to the jack. Your bowl will also slow more quickly as it comes to rest. On a fast green you will need to take a much wider line and your bowl will tend to run on more as it slows down.

In fact, on very fast greens, like New Zealand's cotula surfaces, the bowl almost turns at right angles as it comes to rest.

Although the vast majority of outdoor greens in Britain are grass surfaces, there are synthetic surfaces available and they may well play an important part in the future as maintenance costs of standard greens escalate. Synthetic surfaces tend to be fast and in some ways are more consistent.

Having said that, the nature of the green is variable, and the weather conditions can change not only from game to game but also during the game in progress.

If the grass is not cut reasonably close, it will tend to become flattened during the course of the game and the area where the majority of the play takes place will increase in speed. This is called TRACKING and the longer the game lasts the more difficult the rink will become, not so much in weight but in finding the line. The bowls will tend to hang wide or cut across the head, finishing narrow, which will become more and more exaggerated as the game goes on. This is particularly the case with greens which have not been scarified regularly as they do not dry out and do not provide a firm playing surface.

The main problem that the player faces is that he has to bowl to the outer edge of the worn track to obtain a good line, but if he overgreens he not only finishes wide but drops short as his bowl touches fresh grass that has not been flattened. If he slightly undergreens his bowl he is punished heavily as his delivery invariably cuts away well narrow of the jack.

Such conditions are a great challenge as the arc tends to increase more and more as the match progresses. Here intelligent use of the mat and jack are essential if a bowler is to find both line and length with any regularity.

Moisture on the green will slow it down. If you went onto a green early in the morning when the dew was still on the grass you would find that the drawing arc would be narrower and the pace slower than when the sun dried it off.

The sun will affect the green speed throughout the day. It will be at its most consistent from about mid-day to around six o'clock in the UK.

As the sun sinks the nap on the green lifts in the cooler night air and this will have a slowing effect on the green's surface. When playing in the late afternoon or early evening, there could be a tendency to bowl short, so you must make the appropriate allowances.

On fast greens the draw and the drive will be your most reliable shots. A running shot will be difficult as you will need to be most accurate with your line. Any deviation from the correct line will be punished more on the fast green because of the biasing effect acting more quickly than on a slow green where the effect of bias on the bowl is not so pronounced.

Two other factors will also make a big difference to the way you bowl – wind and rain.

Anxious moments for the author . . . has the speed of the green been judged correctly?

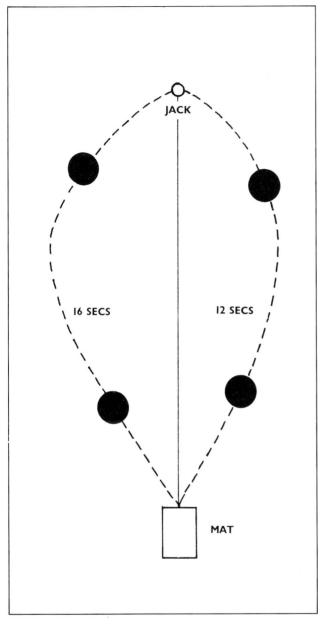

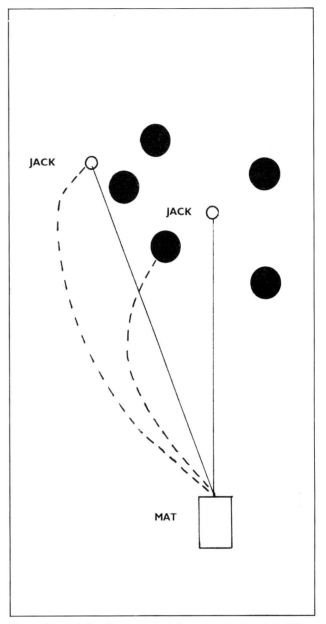

Example of wide and narrow hands. The variation in the amount of 'land' required on certain greens illustrates that length cannot be judged by looking at the jack in a straight line.

The effect of wind on a bowl can be very marked. It may be light or variable, steady, strong or even gusty and each type produces differing conditions.

A light wind will not be too serious a problem but it will still affect the behaviour of your bowls if playing on a fast green. If blowing straight down it will add to the speed of your bowl, when playing with the wind and vice-versa the other way. Bowling with the wind will be difficult as the bowl will tend to run past the jack.

Often the best way to counteract this is to bowl the wider hand to give you better weight.

Bowling into the wind, however, can be far more difficult, particularly on a fast green, as not only is length affected but also line. Finding a consistent green becomes increasingly more difficult the stronger the breeze.

As the greens in the British Isles are usually no faster than 13

Here the jack has been moved from its set position. When drawing to the jack on the edge of the rink, always allow a little extra length and slightly less green to compensate for the slower, less trodden surface, especially outdoors.

seconds, wind does not cause the bowlers as many problems as their counterparts in the southern hemisphere. Undoubtedly the bowls must be affected to some degree but it has to be a very windy day before it becomes so noticeable that it really affects a player's game to the degree of undermining his confidence.

On the faster surfaces of Australia and New Zealand adapting over a game to windy conditions is normal procedure and is even more common to players in these countries than playing in wet conditions is to UK bowlers.

Flag watching is an important part of the game 'down under' and most clubs have pennants in the corners of the green so that the players can determine the direction and strength of the wind, and detect any sudden change.

It is quite fascinating watching these flags as the wind can swirl in different directions on various parts of the green as it is

59

Study of the green

affected by buildings, hedges and stands etc.

But to the players from the southern hemisphere this is an important part of the game which has to be mastered.

Rarely does wind blow directly up and down a rink and more often than not one can expect some degree of crosswind. Generally it is the accepted principle to play the narrow hand in windy conditions, but I do feel that the speed of the green and the wind strength and direction are the main factors that determine the best hand to play.

The worst condition without a doubt is a gusty crosswind which can make even an experienced player look like a complete novice.

I well remember my Commonwealth Games experience in Christchurch, New Zealand, in 1974. Playing under such conditions and on greens running in excess of 20 seconds, like all players I was experiencing difficulty in finding the middle of the rink as no two bowls finished in the same place. This made it very difficult to determine the correct aiming line. All four hands were extremely treacherous and it was not long before I was taking the advice of the locals.

I received many pearls of wisdom but the one piece of advice that I employed to good effect has always stuck in my mind. It is that on a fast green with a gusting crosswind a player is well advised to play the hand where the wind is blowing across his right shoulder and vice-versa, of course, for the left hander.

This I found to be the general opinion of most bowlers when playing on greens of that pace. But playing into the wind there was no real preference as it was generally agreed this was far more difficult.

So to summarise, I believe there is no golden rule as to how one should combat windy conditions as there are so many factors to be taken into consideration. The best yardstick I feel is to play the hand where the bowl is more consistently affected by the wind and if the conditions are gusty, to try and wait just a moment and catch a time when the wind has subsided.

You will not often have to continue to play in very stormy weather but you could well have to play during a short sharp rain shower, or just steady drizzle, and this will again affect your play.

The surface will become sluggish and very heavy, narrowing your line to the jack and forcing you to use more weight. Even if the sun comes out after a shower, this will also have the effect of slowing down the pace of the green as the sun will drag moisture to the surface as it evaporates.

In these conditions it is better to get accustomed early on to at least three-quarter length jacks.

David Rhys-Jones, who has probably played with me more than any other bowler, and I have a policy which we adopt for heavy greens, especially those affected by rain. We always play full-length jacks from the offset so that we don't get caught. If we played short length jacks and our opponents suddenly played a long length, we could easily concede a big count.

Heavy greens are a trial to the player that is used to fast greens. There is always the danger of bowling too many short bowls unless you can find a reasonable length early on.

So tackle the weight problem first and bowl to longer length jacks. Conversely, if playing on a very fast green, short jacks could be your main danger so it would pay to get used to that length early on.

Playing on a bad green is a speciality in itself which demands special tactics.

First of all you must accept the conditions then try to play them to the best of your ability. A really bumpy green that takes little bias will be a problem when short bowls block the head, so when the head gets blocked you must play heavy shots to open it up. It's not so bad on greens that are just heavy and slow. If they are basically level and true you may still be able to draw.

This applies more to team games. In singles play more often than not you must still try to draw the shot.

There are other factors which can affect play, like shadows on the green, particularly late in the afternoon and early evening, cast by trees, the club pavilion or other objects and a variety of 'hills and hollows' to throw your bowls off course. All must be mastered.

Up to now I have dealt with outdoor conditions, now I must turn to indoor.

Fundamentally the two games are the same but, of course, there are seveal practical differences. Indoor the conditions are more regular. The bowler is free from sun, wind, rain and the excessive changes of green pace.

But there are different surfaces and these do have different speeds.

It's true to say that most indoor greens are faster than those experienced outdoor in the UK, but they can have both wide and narrow hands.

There are also 'tricks' indoors, mainly due to problems with the underlay or more probably with the concrete surface below. In Scotland the carpets are often laid on wooden board surfaces which can have 'straights' in them when the wood warps or shrinks giving a crack between joints.

Some surfaces, or at least some underlays, are badly affected by humidity which can also affect the pace and swing of the green. But in general the surfaces are faster and truer running than outdoor.

It would be fair to say that the more experienced bowler can operate with even more success indoor. The moderate bowler may have problems in finding and keeping a length. It is also easier for the skilful bowler to play a variety of weighted shots as there are fewer hazards on the smoother indoor surfaces.

Because the surfaces are faster and there are no problems with moisture, it is possible to bowl with a larger set of bowls indoors. A player who uses a small bowl outdoors could at least go up one size, even two sizes, indoors. Nowadays, however, there are heavyweight bowls, which have the same effect.

The most suitable bowl indoors is the one that takes an average arc to the jack, because you could be bowling down a 'worn' arc as the rinks are often fixed and do not move about as they do outdoors when the greenkeepers move the strings. This again is a form of tracking and certain underlays which compress unevenly are the main cause. Although not so obvious as outdoors, weight variations are experienced, particularly when playing outside the normal line.

Indoors, or out, the draw shot is still the bread and butter shot of bowls. But indoors it is probably more easier to play as the greens are more reliable. So there is just as much need for the running shots, as the heads will be tighter.

However, using running shots indoors can be more difficult, as the faster greens need a more delicate touch. Also bowls move faster out of the head and a lot more can happen.

Sometimes near impossible shots come off.

If you are playing on your own indoor green you will know its little 'tricks', its swing and general characteristics, so you can set the pattern. Away from home you will quickly have to find out what it's all about.

To my mind this is not the case outdoors. Because the greens change so much, ie: the strings have been moved or you are playing the other way on, it is often as difficult for you, as for your opponents.

Some say that outdoor greens are more 'sporty', because you are also playing against the green, but I sometimes think that bad greens and bad weather conditions kill half the pleasure in the game.

After all, if all you want to do is hurl bowls down a green, why not spend an evening at the nearest skittle alley!

I much prefer to play the outdoor game if the conditions are right. Bowling on a good green, on a warm summer day where one can enjoy the exercise and fresh air is definitely much better than spending hours under artificial lighting in a hot stuffy atmosphere.

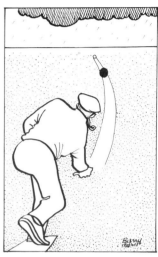

Finding your right line is essential, so watch for any changes in weather conditions during play. Shadows on the green tend to slow down the speed of a green. Wind can also alter both the speed and the amount of draw required on your bowls. Headwinds slow the bowl, following winds speed it up and can turn it into a running bowl. Similarly, crosswinds increase or decrease draw depending on direction. On sunny days you will need to take a wider line to the jack. Under damp and wet conditions your line will be much straighter.

Some points to remember

(1) Are the draws true?
    (i) Do the bowls cut away sharply at the finish?
    (ii) Do the bowls hang off?
    (iii) Do the bowls draw very late?
    (iv) Do the bowls meander?

(2) What is the condition of the green?
    (i) Has it been cut recently?
    (ii) Will it noticeably track and if so to what degree?
    (iii) Are both sides of the rink running at the same speed?
    (iv) Does the rink play at the same pace both ways?
    (v) Is the texture of the grass even?
    (vi) Are there any areas with tricks, subtle or marked?
    (vii) Are there any areas where the bowls pick up speed? Are the ends faster?
    (viii) Are there any worn areas?
    (ix) Are there any other hazards:
        (a) Is it bumpy?
        (b) Is it wet and slippery?
        (c) Is it very uneven?
        (d) Is the wind affecting play?
        (e) Are the conditions likely to change during the game?
    (x) Do the banks and ditches conform?
        (a) Will the jack or bowl rebound?
        (b) Will the jack or bowl jump the bank?
        (c) Is the ditch of a holding nature?

(3) Assess pace and work out type of game to suit the prevailing conditions.
(4) Quickly establish line and work out the best hands for the draw, running bowls, the drive, etc.

Use of mat and jack

Placing the mat is quite simple, but do it correctly, not one-handed. Make sure (above) that you grip the front edge of the mat with your back to the rink and line-up the centre of the mat with the rink marker (below) with the front edge you are gripping not less than six feet from the edge of the ditch (See Laws of the game).

Make good use of them – they're so important

There can be no question that good use of both the mat and the jack is extremely important in the game of bowls. And they are both inseparable.

Basically, you stand on the mat to deliver your bowl and the jack is the target at which play is directed round.

The right to roll the jack on the first end is decided by the toss of a coin in most cases of competitive play. The position of the mat under IBB law is fixed on the first end, the front edge of the mat being six feet from the front edge of the ditch.

After that, providing that the jack is 25 yards from the front edge of the mat and no less than six feet from the front of the ditch, you may move the mat up and down the green.

The position of the jack on the green determines the distance over which players must deliver their bowls. So you can see that if you are able to control this distance by learning the art of rolling the jack, you have taken an important step to becoming a successful bowler.

The mat may be a very simple piece of equipment, but it should be regarded as more than just a passive instrument. The mat can work for you as an aid to winning ends, so make sure that you lay it with care.

The actual mechanics of laying the mat are quite simple.

Facing the ditch, with your back to the rink and grasping the front edge of the mat, you will lay it along the centre-line of the rink. In this country we do not usually mark the centre of the rink so you have to rely on the rink marker.

Check that the mat is centred properly, especially if you have taken it well up the green. Your marker in singles or your skip in team games will tell you if you are not sure.

Although this seems a simple task it is very important. Successful play in bowls stems from the ability to be able to

read with your eyes the green line to take and you will use your mat to position your feet. So if the mat is NOT correctly positioned your estimations could be affected.

In level green bowls, the jack is not biased like the bowl and will roll from the mat in a straight line. It should be delivered (or rolled) in much the same way as a bowl. There are still too many players who just seem to throw the jack up the green and then turn their backs on it. Although it is much smaller and considerably less heavier than a bowl, dropped on the green it can still mark it.

A lot of players are unable to control either the length or direction when casting the jack. There is nothing worse than seeing a lead rolling the jack into the next rink. Besides being a poor effort, he also forfeits the right to determine the jack length on that end.

The importance of being able to roll the jack in a straight line to a determined length cannot be over emphasised. Once you have mastered the ability to control the length of the jack, you have gained a distinct advantage.

The grip should be the same as for a bowl, although because of the size it will be more in the tips of the fingers than in the palm of the hand.

Players who adopt the 'cradle' style of delivery will, perhaps, have a tendency to bowl the jack from the palm as well and this often causes the jack to go off centre.

You should stand on the mat in much the same manner as for playing the draw shot, facing your line with your feet. As this line is straight down the middle of the rink, then your feet

Deliver the jack from the tips of the fingers (left) even if you use a cradle grip - there's less tendency for the jack to go off line - making sure to face your line with your feet (above).

Use of mat and jack

will obviously be pointing in that direction towards the far rink marker.

Roll the jack with a smooth flowing action with the delivery hand following through palm upwards.

Although, as I have said before, the jack isn't biased, nevertheless a few tips can be gleaned from its movement up the green. If the green is fast it will roll easily, likewise it will pull up if slow. Bumps and dips can be noticed sometimes from the movement of the jack.

I think at this stage I should discuss the slightly controversial subject of whether or not to hold a bowl while delivering the jack.

The majority of experts I have discussed this with are divided as to whether you should attempt to deliver the jack with a bowl in your other hand.

I NEVER do, much preferring to place the bowl alongside the mat.

I don't personally agree with the explanation given for picking up the bowl at the same time as the jack, that you subconsciously retain the feeling of length and having to pick up a bowl will disturb the continuity. But some players do and it works for them.

Another controversial decision is whether to take the jack if you win the toss on the first end. As you have only played two trial ends you cannot really play to a length where you will be certain of gaining any advantage and therefore it is perhaps better to deliver the last bowl, hopefully converting the head.

In team play, particularly triples and fours, I would definitely favour the latter, as unless I have a pre-conceived plan the jack has no particular significance as far as I am concerned and the mat is fixed two yards from the ditch anyway.

However, in singles there is a good argument for taking the jack as usually all four bowls are used on trial ends which gives players more idea of the reliability of the hands and the pace of the green. Usually the man who bowls the first bowl close to the jack dictates the end so therefore the player who bowls first plays two out of the first three bowls and obviously stands the better chance of getting in first.

In the situation of a game going to an extra end, many factors have to be considered. If there is no real marked advantage on any given length, always bearing in mind that the mat is in a fixed position two yards from the ditch, there is a strong argument for settling for the last bowl and giving the jack to your opponents.

On the other hand, if your team show a marked superiority over a certain distance then the opportunity of playing to that length, I feel, far outweighs the advantage of bowling the last bowl which would be under extreme pressure anyway.

Always remember that the jack should be delivered to a length which suits the team and not the individual, and that it pays not only to play to your strength but also to your opponents' weakness.

Four shots scored inches from the jack are exactly the same as four scored from several feet away when they go on the card. Although your team may not be very happy on a tricky length, as long as you are scoring and playing the green marginally better than your opponents it's good tactics. Never change a winning length.

If playing inexperienced bowlers it is often good tactics to place the jack as near to the end of the green as possible irrespective of the position of the mat on the green. Inexperienced bowlers are usually afraid of going into the

When asking the marker or skip to position the jack on the centre line, give clear, deliberate instructions, don't simply wag an index finger in

front of your nose. And if you are placing the jack for a team-mate do it by hand, NOT with the sole of your shoe, as you're likely to obscure the

centre line marker and possibly damage the green, too.

DON'T deliver the jack with both feet on the mat like this, you will not be able to bowl it accurately.

DON'T deliver the jack while holding your bowl away from the body, it will tend to put you off balance.

This is acceptable, but personally I never deliver the jack with my first bowl in my hand.

ditch and have a tendency to drop their bowls short if this tactic is employed.

But when playing against an experienced bowler with a good firm shot or drive it is often best to leave plenty of room between the jack and the ditch so that in the event of the jack being moved there will still be room for the draw shot.

All of this stresses once more the importance of being able to bowl the jack with accuracy. And as far as I am concerned there is only one way to deliver a jack and that is correctly as described.

Having covered how to use the jack we can now turn to discuss more thoroughly the advantages to be gained by making good use of the mat.

It must be remembered that when changing the length of the jack it is also advisable to alter the position of the mat. This will force changes in the land that the bowls will have to take. By moving the mat up the green you can vary the conditions.

This is important when you are playing a green that is tracking. That is when, if your line is not absolutely accurate, bowls will cut across the head or hang out. By moving the mat up the green you should be able to find the middle of the rink much better.

You will see that an experienced player makes good use of the mat for THREE main reasons.

● To alter the position along the centre of the green to avoid any peculiarities or at least reduce their effects.

● To alter feet positions in order to play either a narrow or wide bowl to miss another bowl that may be in the drawline.

● To alter the mat position along the centreline in order to secure an advantage over an opponent.

You will soon see that by moving the mat up and down the green how imperfections in the green's surface can be avoided. And this applies both indoor and outdoor, although you tend to expect more imperfections on outdoor surfaces.

If your opponents are scoring particularly well on a jack length then as soon as you win an end change the length. Then if this length suits you – stick to it.

It is much easier to play to a certain length of jack with the mat in a certain position if it works for you. Even if you lose an end in between, return to that length next time round.

Remember as well that no green is the same all over and sometimes bad patches can act to your advantage. If you are handling them better than your opponents, keep persevering. Having a left-hander in your team can also be a great advantage on an awkward green.

You can get a different line to the jack by delivering from either the inside or the outside of the mat and a lot of bowlers use this tactic for drawing round a bowl, or getting inside one. Similarly some bowlers, although I think very few, will deliver off the front or the back of the mat. In other words if they are say 18ins heavy with a bowl, they will then step back and deliver from the back of the mat to make the adjustment for drawing to the right spot.

Personally I am not very keen on this, although I do use the inside of the mat sometimes as a last resort.

The danger of stepping back on the mat, particularly on a fast green, is that you would be grounding your bowl

Use of mat and jack

dangerously close to the front edge of the mat.

I am personally a great believer in delivering your bowls from the same place on the mat every time, unless you really know the green. Then the line to be taken will be very apparent to you and you will be able to pick it out straight away without thinking every time you step on the mat.

When you have that sort of confidence, then perhaps you can start playing around with where you stand on the mat.

The question is often posed, who should determine the jack length, the skip or the lead? I always give my leads the choice in the early stages of the game and rarely interfere until I have worked out the general tactics of the game. Then if I want to change a jack length I do so in consultation with my team.

The skip, however, should always be aware of where he wants the jack.

There is not much point if your lead is finding a particular length but nobody else in the team is, in sticking to that position, especially if your opponents are finding it.

But normally a good skip will only dictate a jack length if he has a particular reason to do so.

Often it's a good tactical ploy to bring the mat up the green, but you'll need the marker or your skip to make sure it's straight. This is about half-a-mat away from lining up with the number on the bank.

If the green is heavy I would tend to ask for a full-length jack to begin with in order to sample the green at its worst. On an average-paced green, I would be quite happy to let my lead dictate the length. I wouldn't expect him to bowl a short jack, however, on the first end.

The beauty of a long jack to begin with is that you will be able to determine the maximum draw straight away. Rarely do you find that a hand on a green will swing more to a short length jack than to a long.

Movement of the mat and jack are very important to setting the pace of a match and games can be won by good use. I am a great believer in taking the mat up the green when I'm in trouble. Very often the most drastic measures work and very often your opponent's rhythm can be upset, firstly by moving the mat and then when returning to the previous length that he had been successful on.

So when you have got a smooth delivery with your bowls, practice casting the jack accurately and to different lengths.

Some points to remember . . .

THE JACK

(1) The Jack should be delivered with care. It should be bowled not thrown.
(2) The jack should be positioned to suit the team and not the individual.
(3) Remember that it not only pays to play to your strength but also to your opponent's weakness. What suits you may suit them but a length of jack which you do not particularly like may cause them far greater problems.
(4) Are there any left-handers on the rink? Because of the different grounding position of the bowl their influence can have a great affect on the game and should be considered when deciding on the length of the jack.

THE MAT

(1) Just as changing the length of jack has a marked effect on a game so, too, does movement of the mat. In actual fact it is more effective in as much that players not only have to adjust weight but also have to alter line slightly according to how far it is moved up the green.
(2) It is the lead's job to always remember exactly where he has placed the mat on previous ends.
(3) Remember no two twenty-five yard jacks will bowl the same, as the mat position can vary by eleven yards. The extremes will vary considerably in line and weight and often, with the mat well up the green, certain irregularities show up on the playing surface.
(4) When a green is tracking badly and players are experiencing great difficulty in finding the centre, astute positioning of the mat can easily overcome the problem. Moving the mat several yards up the green and bowling to the same mark increases the angle from the mat yet still allows the bowl to travel down the worn path, greatly reducing the cut away over the final two yards. As the tracking increases as the game progresses, further movement of the mat may be necessary.

An instance where I used the mat to good advantage. This is the Kodak Masters in 1982, when I brought the mat up the green to shake South African Bill Moseley off his length . . . and it succeeded.

Choice of hand

There's so much to learn from the opening ends

There are several points that you are going to have to learn about during the opening ends of any bowls match. And your success is going to rely on how quickly you learn to read your green in those opening stages.

I never think it's a bad idea to give the mat to your opponent if you win the toss. Invariably he will cast the jack to a length that suits him. This isn't a bad thing because it will enable you

One of the most deadly sins in bowls is the jack-high bowl of which white has played two, here. Though they are close to the jack they can be easily wrested. But black should avoid the tendency to play a running bowl, better results can be obtained with a well greened draw shot.

The black bowls, meanwhile, are well placed as they present a small target to white and from the mat, the distance between mat and jack are hard to determine.

to work out his strengths early in the game.

Also, having the last bowl on the first end is never detrimental as nobody knows exactly what length they want at that stage, so you may be able to cash-in without showing all your aces straight away.

Experiment for the first couple of ends to find the best side of the rink and mainly try to stick to it.

Sometimes a lead might be able to bowl one side better, his No.2 the other (particularly if he is left-handed) BUT I'm a great believer in keeping my lead and No.2 on the same hand nearly all the time although they may be playing different sides of the rink.

If you keep playing one side of the green you get to know it better and better, and really the task of those two players in a game of fours is to build up the head. It's better to have four bowls in the head, even if you haven't got the shot. You must try to pressurise your opponents into playing the worst sides of a rink.

The value of a good lead cannot be over-emphasised and many times, if a lead is bowling well, you will go on to win. But a lead can still bowl well and find himself on the losing side.

One thing that is certain in bowls – consistency counts.

To some degree it is better for a lead to have a bowl 18" from the jack and the other two feet short, than one 6" from the jack and the other three yards short.

Bowls in the head are what count the most. If your opponent puts a bowl fairly close to the jack, then your aim will be to try and beat this bowl to gain shot. But if you hit that bowl into the head, don't be disappointed because with more bowls in the head there is always the possibility that you can get the shot second time around from the bowl that you have played up.

If that is the only bowl that your opposition has in the head then they could well be in trouble, because you can remove it for a big count.

And if you have several close seconds, you can always go for the conversion shot with confidence.

The bowl that is always a menace is the jack high bowl as it is so vulnerable. This is why it is important to find the right line to the jack early on in the game. A bowl that is there or thereabouts on line behind the jack or in front is always useful. If your bowl is at jack high length but about a yard from the jack it is of very little use. Perhaps on a fast green the jack might be sliced sideways, but certainly never on slower greens.

Even if a jack was cut across on a slow green it probably wouldn't travel very far. So remember – jack high bowls are taboo, usually someone will rest them.

On heavy greens try not to be short. Short bowls on heavy greens are fatal. They are difficult to get round because if the green is heavy the line to the jack will be narrower, and if increased weight is added to get round the short bowls there is a tendency for them to stay out and not be able to bias enough to come into the head.

In the early stages of a match it is a good thing to watch your opponents bowls to see how they behave – BUT DO NOT AUTOMATICALLY FOLLOW THEM. His bowls will most probably act slightly differently to yours, they may be a wider-drawing bowl or narrower, different size and weight, so will not act in the same way.

You can, of course, use your knowledge of his bowls to your advantage.

If you have noticed that his bowls are taking a much wider

line to the jack than yours and it is a fast green, you may decide to play longer jacks on the principle that he will need a very wide draw to reach his objective. Conversely, on the shorter jack you may find that your bowls pick up the straighter runs but your opponent's wide-drawing bowls come across them.

So there are advantages and disadvantages in the type of bowls you may be playing with on particular greens.

I am sure that in time the top players will use particular bowls for particular greens if they happen to know how they react, carrying three of four sets with them just like top tennis players have their special rackets or snooker men their cues.

Remember the trial ends can be very useful to a player not only to see how his own bowls behave, but also to assess the strengths and weaknesses of his opponent. This is particularly true of singles play, although even in pairs, triples or fours he should be watching his opposite number.

You should quickly work out the best length of jack to suit you or your team, and remember that if your bowls are finishing in the middle of the green then you are obviously finding the right line. It just needs weight adjustment then to get the right length.

Many games are won by good draw play and many are lost by poor shots made when the opportunity was wide open to add to the score. Six easy shots played carelessly can make all the difference to winning or losing.

Some points to remember . . .

(1) Contrary to common belief the shortest way to the jack is not always the best. More often than not it is, but a player should always be looking for the hand which gives him the highest percentage of bowls on the centre line.

(2) Bowls twelve inches or less directly in line in front or behind the jack are excellent, but bowls approximately jack high (say 6 inches either way) are unfortunate deliveries and there to be wrested. Remember straight heads win matches.

(3) It is usually beneficial to play one side of the rink both ways – that is backhand up and forehand down the rink. This is because, more often than not, there is a variation in pace on the two sides of the green. However, common sense must prevail and if the two backhands or two forehands are the only reliable ways to the jack the adjustment of weight is probably far easier to overcome than unpredictable lines on the unreliable hands.

(4) A player must always appreciate the importance of good line. If he is certain that he can deliver his bowl to finish on the centre line consistently, he will become more confident. However, the most important factor is that when he takes his stance on the mat, having lined himself up, his whole concentration will be on WEIGHT. When a player has a niggling doubt as to whether he will hit his line his weight is bound to suffer as his concentration is divided.

(5) Remember rarely do two sets of bowls take an identical line. Variations of size, weight, shape, material, and delivery action are the obvious reasons and therefore what suits one player may not suit another. How often I have heard a player say "I could not find that hand at all!" Whereas all the other bowlers on the rink had played it well.

(6) Watch carefully not only where your team bowls finish but those of your opponents. Choice of hand, placement of mat, position of jack etc. may well be governed by this.

Below: When playing on ditch or end rinks – this is the Leamington venue for the English women's championships – keep playing on one side both ways where possible. Seldom is a ditch rink the same speed on two sides, indeed the ditch side is usually faster particularly outdoors because of the wear it receives when the rinks are switched at right-angles.

Position and impact of bowls

Here is a typical plant situation (above left). My opponent has three bowls in front of the jack and one a few inches directly behind. My white bowls are well placed for me to come up with my last bowl and cannon into my bowls on the line to the jack and spring my nearest shot into my opponent's bowl alongside the jack. As you can see (above right), this has brought me at least three shots.

Why you need a snooker player's knowledge

Tactics will vary according to the pace of the green.

When the green is heavy it is essential to get bowls into the head. Don't worry particularly who has shot in the early stages and remember that short bowls are wasted on heavy greens. The last two or three bowls will invariably settle the issue.

The faster the surface the more unpredictable will be the end result if a jack is moved. On a fast green there will be a lot of movement after a heavy bowl enters the head; the jack may get sliced sideways or off the green and other bowls will be driven out. On heavier greens the effect is often less dramatic. The jack just goes back and bowls stop dead.

Medium-paced greens will present you with the most difficulties. You will need a wide variety of shots which will often be difficult to calculate.

In team play more conversion shots are played, therefore the wise skip always ensures that he has got plenty of cover at the back of the head while he is lying with close shots.

It is as well to remember that packing the head with bowls isn't a good idea. The more packed the head the greater target it becomes and often the bigger the eventual loss.

I spoke earlier of the movement of bowls and the jack when driving or even when yard-on shots are played. Any good bowler should have the knowledge of what happens to bowls when they are struck.

A bowler needs knowledge similar to that of the top snooker players. And I draw this analogy deliberately because I think the two games are very similar.

The bowler has to recognise how to play a 'plant' shot – hitting one bowl against another to achieve his objective. He needs to know what will happen when he hits one against another, or even two or three. And he has to recognise that bowls have a 'running' and 'check' side as indeed snooker balls do.

The snooker player achieves his 'bias' by cueing the balls with either top, bottom or side spin. This has the effect of rolling balls on, stopping them dead or slicing them to get wider or narrower angles and into position for another shot.

This is the same in bowls except that you use the bowl's natural bias to achieve the objective.

Say there is a bowl in the middle of the rink that you want to

Right: Bowling on a fast surface, where there will be a lot of movement if a bowl is played into a head. As you will see from the white shoes, this was in Australia – the 1981 Mazda 'Jack High' Masters in Melbourne.

Position and impact of bowls

The pictures left and centre illustrate how a bowl is played with 'check' side, rebounding against the bias, from a bowl to take the shot. Here my bowl is played with a little extra weight into the middle bowl of a cluster of opposition bowls in order to straighten and take the shot. The right-hand picture simply illustrates the shot played with 'running side' –

play. If you hit that bowl playing a backhand shot on the left-hand side, your bowl will come off and travel down the middle of the rink in a straight line. If you hit it going away on the right-hand side the bias will be acting with it and will take the bowl on more or less a horizontal line across the green.

Now I would refer to the first bowl as being played on the check side, the second one on the running side.

You can get the angle from a bowl playing on either hand, straight or at right angles, according to the pace of the green. If you have a wide-drawing green you can get bowls to come off at all angles from the bowl that you hit by using variations of weight and varying thickness of contact with the object bowl.

This is where the real skill in bowls comes in – being able to play a shot with specific weight and green to angle correctly off

to quote a snooker term – where my bowl comes in, nudging off the centre of the three bowls to knock the jack into my own back bowls for a possible count of three. This is a 'cannon with the bias'.

a bowl on contact. You will then have to think of the thickness of that contact.

To gain any angle you will have to come off a bowl by striking it on one-half of its surface or less. Any fuller would merely play that bowl up into the head and would be more of a follow through shot.

So here judgement of weight and the right green will be crucial.

We often speak of weight and sometimes it is an elusive thing. Yet it is the one factor that makes the difference between the average bowler and the top-class bowler. Judgement of weight is bound up with correct sighting and finding the right land. It is also the most difficult factor in bowls to master. Never forget that mastery of all shots stems from

Position and impact of bowls

knowing the weight of the green and therefore good length play.

Weight is particularly important with the firm shots – wicks, cannons and plants – so it is very important to study the effects of bowl on bowl so that you can perfect the right angles.

Always remember that the bowls will react differently on slow to fast greens.

So to summarise:
1. Be consistent.
2. Avoid playing jack high bowls.
3. Don't always try to get shot. Remember that bowls in the head are just as important.
4. Master your line first and foremost.
5. Assess your opponent's strength and weaknesses.
6. Find out which hand of the green suits you best – and stick to it.
7. Remember short bowls on heavy greens are wasted.

Some points to remember . . .

(1) Are you a billiards or snooker player? If so you will already have an insight into the many variations that are possible in most heads.
(2) Become a player who studies the head very carefully and who does not always decide to play the obvious shot or the first shot that springs to mind.
(3) Always consider your opponent. What will he be attempting?
(4) Be familiar with:
    (a) Plants or Sets.
    (b) Cannons with the bias.
    (c) Cannons against the bias.
    (d) Run throughs.
    (e) Wicks and multiple wicks.
    (f) Splits.
    (g) Front cover shots.

Below: A typical situation for the cannon bowl. Here with my World championship triples partner Jimmy Hobday (second from the left), we discuss the possibilities of a tight head.

If you are a billiards or snooker player like me you will no doubt have an insight into the action of balls cannoning into other balls and the angles at which they deflect. Many of the same rules apply with bowls.

The head - choice of shot

Calculating the odds, selecting the moment

There are many points to consider during an end of bowls with regard to the state of the head at a given time and the choice of shot that is open to the player on the mat.

In this chapter I am going to deal with the choice left for a skip, or what a skip will ask his other players to do and what you should be thinking about during a singles game.

The four main questions to ask yourself are:
● What do I stand to gain?
● What do I stand to lose?
● What are the chances of it going against me?
● Is this the time to play it?

We are, therefore, looking at the shot in a percentage situation.

In selecting the shot to play the player has to assess his chances. That is, if he is slightly overweight he can wick off a bowl, rest the shot bowl, trail the jack or finish in a useful position. In addition he cannot take his nearest bowl out as it is well covered. He also has to estimate his chances of success which may well be 50/50.

However, if when he poses the question 'What are the chances of it going against me?' he feels that at best he can score two but if he has an accident he could drop five then the overall percentages are against him. Had the situation been in reverse, and he could go from one down to two down but equally have the chance of collecting five, then there would be every incentive for him to play the shot.

Another point he must consider is 'Is this the time to play it?'

It is most important to take a look at the scorecard and in team games, such as the international matches or Middleton Cup, you must look at the overall picture when playing certain shots. The last thing that you want to do is try some trick shot at a crucial stage in the game.

If you are going to take chances, and as anyone knows who has played with me I'm not averse to having a go provided they are calculated chances, the time for such shots is in the first 12 ends.

In other words if the chance presents itself in the first 12 ends to get a big count then that's not a bad time to try, particularly if you are two or three shots up at the time. If it goes wrong then you are still in the match, and if your shot comes off the gap between your score and your opponent's will widen. If you get to the last third of a match with around six shots to spare, you would then be looking to score on just two or three of the last five ends to make sure of victory.

In other words, put up the shutters in the last seven ends.

A lot of players try to be too greedy in the last third of a match by going for shots that they don't really need. Remember it's better to have two good shots on the jack and a perfect position than to move the jack a little and score five but leave the jack in a position that your opposing skip can exploit.

You put it into the open – he comes down and slams it into the ditch and what price your five shots then? He could well score out of that end, which he possibly wouldn't have done if you had not moved it.

Study of the head to forecast the likely outcome of any shot is a vital part of successful play.

If you have shot against you and as one of the two skips you go down to play first, you have got to look carefully if it pays you to get the shot or not!

Now that might sound a little Irish, but sometimes in getting the shot you might by moving the jack give your opponent a better chance of a bigger count than he had before. If he gets that count you are then left with a situation where you each have one bowl left. The pressure is really on you. You may get the shot back, but he still has last bowl and can take you out again to regain his big count.

And if you should miss, well he just has to put his last bowl in for yet another shot.

There is no need to put yourself under pressure. Sometimes it is better to be one down and relatively safe than to try any heroics when position is against you.

Similarly, if you are one down and he has the two best back bowls – think carefully before you choose to play a firing shot. If your bowl doesn't go through with the jack on the trail and the jack goes through to the back of the head, even into the ditch, then you are in trouble.

He has two shots and can draw another. Left with a bowl each, and remember it's your last, you have got to succeed. If you go into the ditch you're three down and he has every chance of drawing a fourth.

So you have lost a four, although in the first place you were only one shot down and your opponent was in a position where it was perhaps difficult for him to get another shot. In this case you would find it better to leave him with just that one shot.

The head - choice of shot

I never like forcing the jack into the open with my first bowl as skip when my opponent has got two bowls to my one out of the last three bowls to be played.

You have always got to remember – especially if you have been winning most of the ends – that your opposing skip will have two out of the last three bowls and have two bites at the cherry.

It can also happen (particularly on a woolly green) that you will have to play out of line on some fresh grass and risk a big count. I'm always very wary, particularly on British outdoor greens (it's not so bad indoors) when the jack goes in the ditch.

If you have to go out to the strings and your opponent has the last bowl, it's alright if you have the shots. He can draw two or you can draw another one. But if they are actually lying when the jack goes in the ditch and he draws another with one to play you have to be very sure with that last bowl.

He might have shot four feet from the ditch and third and fourth shots as much as eight/.10 feet away. But you dare not lose your bowl – just play to beat the second and third shots.

If you do that, he can still draw another, but that is better than losing double the amount of shots.

'Is it the right time?' is a question that is often ignored by many players.

Another point when you are considering driving in the early part of the game, and many people do play running shots in the first few ends, is whether or not that is really the right time to play running shots?

Personally I don't like playing running shots and drives in the first five ends. I'm a great believer in the fact that if you have to play them then do so – but if you can avoid playing running shots early it is more desirable.

In the first five ends, when you are struggling to get a length, the green is changing so the last thing you want to do is upset your rhythm by introducing more variables.

When you play your first few bowls it helps to roll the green down and it may have a bit of bite to begin with before settling to a moderate pace. But if you are having to play running shots each time that you go on the mat in the opening ends you are not going to be able to judge what pace it is.

It has happened to me where I have been playing running shots early in the match and suddenly been confronted with a situation where the jack has gone out into the open and I'm about four down with seven feet to draw in and failed. So all the good I've done in those previous ends has been counteracted because I failed to draw within about six feet of the jack. That was because I hadn't had to draw a bowl for about four ends and the pace of the green had changed.

The green can speed up by two to three yards after six ends and you are still playing the pace the same as in the trial ends.

Trial ends are very important for getting the line. You want to find out a good line, even if you pick the wrong hand. Although you might find that you cannot get a line when it changes, at least you've found the pace of the green.

On the whole I have a positive approach to play and am somewhat more concerned with the things I am attempting to do than with frustrating the opponent. However, that does not mean I like to present opponents with simple targets, and the bowl six inches in front of the jack is far less vulnerable than one either side of it or just at the back.

If a bowl is good and occupying a desired position my objective is to follow it up with a second. This should be easier

An accurate backhand trail could score white seven shots and an opportunity such as this in the first two thirds of a match must be attempted. However, if white was five shots up and playing the 18th end a mistake could prove a disaster and his lead might be cut to a couple of shots. Therefore it might be sensible to draw for another shot or even take one.

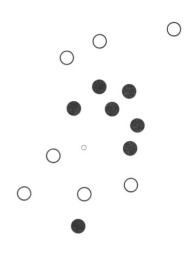

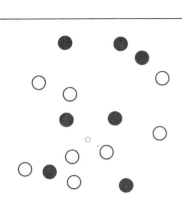

Black has the last bowl to play and is one down. Here we have a perfect example of everything to gain and little to lose. A backhand delivery with sufficient weight to take out the shot bowl or trail the jack (or both) could materialise into a count of six or seven shots. The worst that could happen, if the bowl is correctly weighted, is for the jack to find its way through to white's back bowls and concede two shots. Therefore the percentages are right with a high chance of success.

Black is two down and has the last bowl to play. Here we have a classic example of when to play the firm bowl or drive. Already two down and with four black bowls in the head there is little likelihood of being worse off if the shot is badly played. However, if the jack is successfully ditched there is every chance of scoring four shots. The forehand is the best to play as there is more margin for error.

The head - choice of shot

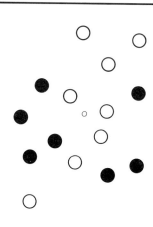

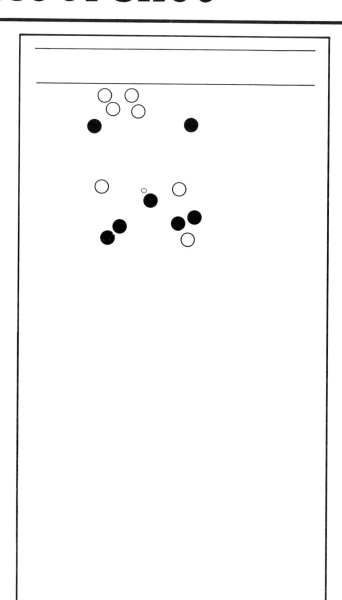

Black's first consideration must be to save, yet the three best back bowls are against him. He really has two options. Either he can fire hoping to clear out some of the shots and gambling that the jack will not move or he can play a yard of weight on his forehand across the head endeavouring to catch his short bowl going away or even inch off one bowl onto the other, eventually turning it in to save or even score shot.

Here is an occasion to use a heavy bowl to gain a count of four. White plays on to the black toucher to spring the jack towards the cluster of white bowls near the ditch.

because the line of approach has already been discovered and another bowl down that line and of similar strength to the first should drop on it. Clearly if the first bowl has gone astray then you would seek to put it right with the second.

Don't try the dramatic. Concentrate all your attention and effort on getting as near as possible to the shot bowl or to getting the best safety position for your team. Success means at worse a good second and at best a position that can be improved without too much in the way of exceptional skill.

The way in which anyone attempts to play a certain shot, or the strength it should be given, form another question. Every shot has its perfect strength, but it may well be a toss-up whether or not it is advisable to play it at its perfect strength or with a little extra weight.

One has a strength which is easiest to play, which you find most comfortable and natural. It may be fast, medium or even just over a draw. This is true for every bowler and it applies for coming on to another bowl.

Sometimes if you are playing a shot and it imparts just the right strength to wrest out a bowl, it may also carry the jack to score more shots. On the other hand it may be so vital to get the shot that the prospect of scoring more shots is relatively unimportant.

It is all a question of priorities. If you are up by about eight shots and there is the chance of ditching the jack for another six or an easy draw for a single, you may well decide to go for the six because that would probably put your match beyond doubt.

There are no hard and fast rules, only the four questions that I posed at the beginning.

A good example of this thinking occured during my final against John Scadgell in the 1965 national indoor singles championship. The match had scarcely begun and I had three scoring bowls slightly in front and to the right of the jack. John had a couple out of harm's way and one diagonally behind the jack by about a yard.

The obvious course was to bowl my fourth bowl alongside his back position for protection. Instead I bowled it into my three, deliberately leaving the jack exposed, reasoning that he must go for the jack but under pressure would hopefully miss. On the other hand, if he caught the jack the most he would score was two and if he was fractionally overstrength he might

push the jack over the 'strings' for a replay of the end.

The best laid schemes, however, can come unstuck. John picked up the jack strongly, only for it to rebound off his own back bowl into my four instead of running dead or scoring two for him.

So my principle had worked out, although not in the way I had imagined. But my assessment of the percentages had been corrrect and if you stick with that, you nearly always win even when luck enters into it.

Points to remember:
(1) Drawing is not the only way of saving shots – driving can be equally effective. The position of the bowls and the distance from the jack should be the decisive factor in making up your mind which is the right shot to play.
(2) When several shots down with the chance of a count, which is the main priority – saving or converting? Saving may require a far easier shot and the temptation of going for a count perhaps should be resisted. Careful consideration of the state of the game, knowledge of the hand, the degree of difficulty of the shot etc. should be coolly calculated before stepping on to the mat.
(3) Playing a very difficult and highly ambitious shot as opposed to an easier one is only justified when failure means the loss of a single shot and success means a count.
(4) Never lose sight of who has to deliver two out of the last three bowls. If shot is against you and your opponent has two bowls after your initial delivery any movement of the jack must be carefully contemplated. Conversely, when the position is reversed and the head is in your favour after the opposing skip's first delivery, all possibilities should be reviewed.
(5) Try to refrain from playing too many running shots in the early stages of a game or you may regret it in the latter stages. Instead, concentrate on perfecting line and mastering the weight of the green.
(6) Look for shots in the first two thirds of the game and, if successful, play it tight during the last six or seven ends. If you are shots up at the 14 to 15 ends stage your opponents may well have to chance their arm. Scoring on two or three of the remaining ends will surely be sufficient.

This was Swansea 1967 when Bryant captained England for the International Series. "It's most important during matches like Middleton Cup or internationals to look at the overall picture when playing certain shots," he says.

Singles play

Consistency – the key to singles success

A singles match has always been, and will always remain, the biggest drawcard in bowls. Like with many sports it is the man-to-man confrontation that always provides the best spectacle.

That is why televised bowls nearly always features singles matches because this is what the viewing audience prefers to watch.

The players pitting their individual skills on the arena. It's as old as time – caveman against the mammoth, the Roman chariot race and the early Olympic Games, they were all the same spectacle.

If you are ambitious, then success in singles will ensure that you gain a much surer step on the ladder. It is also the feeling of controlling your own destiny, being out on your own and being able to play the shots that YOU want that appeals to the more competitively minded players.

If you win then it's a personal glory, if you lose there can be no recriminations except against yourself.

Although it is still only a small percentage of bowls players who enter tournaments, many other players enjoy competitions at club level and the numbers are rising rapidly each year.

Singles play is one of the best ways for any player to improve his game. It provides the type of experience a player needs to perfect his armoury of shots, improve his confidence (especially if he can keep winning) and will help to formulate that most important characteristic – temperament.

It is probably from the ranks of the top singles players that most national teams are picked.

A good singles player is probably a bowler who has mastered every position on the rink, not just at lead. He will have based his skill on the draw shot, which is the foundation stone of the singles game, and progressed by putting all the other shots in his locker.

He will have learned that the firm shot is one of his most valuable assets, especially if the run of the green is against him. And he will have collected a series of 'Dos' and 'Don'ts' which will be invaluable as time goes on.

Earlier on I mentioned that one of the most important aspects of a bowler's play was temperament. As I will be dealing with this subject in full in the next chapter there is no need for me to expand on this much further other than to say that, while it might take just a few years for a player to play shots pretty efficiently, it can take much longer to school your temperament to take the strain of championship play.

Always remember that many bowlers, including top-class players, have been beaten because they were lacking in this department.

Your first championship win, even if it's just a club handicap competition, will give you a lot of confidence which you can build on.

In playing singles there are some important points to remember. These are points that have cropped-up over many years and behind them is the weight of expert opinion coupled with a good deal of common sense. So I will go through them

When assessing the head ask yourself, "What do I stand to gain or lose? What is the state of the game? Is this the time to play it?

with you and try at the same time to give my personal advice.

If you win the toss, should you play first?

Now there are many theories about this both for and against. Some say that you should play first, thus dictating the opening length, others that you should let your opponent start, giving yourself the last bowl. I think it matters very little at the start of a match.

Both mat placement and jack length are of paramount importance. Throwing the jack can determine the pace of the end. After the first few ends you will also have determined what length of jack your opponent prefers. So you will want to play not only to your strengths, but to his weaknesses as well. Never vary a length while you are winning, but if you find that

Right: Receiving the CIS Singles trophy at Wymondham Dell in 1982 after demoralising Brenden McBrien in the final.

Below: In action against my old singles adversary David McGill of Scotland.

Singles play

your opponent is also playing that length well then change it for a while before returning back to your favourite length. Always calculate to a yard the length of jack you are playing to. Length can be estimated by the distance past the 27 yard markers and the distance from the back of the green – if you know the length of the green.

Experiment on the trial ends and on the first few ends to find the best hand, and only change from this hand when it suits you. NEVER try and master a bad hand. Better to play the easier hand even if you have a bowl in the draw. It is better to lose the occasional point than try to conquer an erratic hand.

Your first two bowls into the head are the all important ones. Play those well and you will have the confidence to be successful with your next two bowls. It is all important to get your first bowl close to the jack, always remembering that a jack high bowl 6"-12" from the jack is the worst bowl possible and will rarely be held against a good class bowler. If your rival plays short of the jack try hard to get closer. If you succeed you are well on the way to winning the head. The pressure you then put on your opponent is often enough to make him over-correct and bowl through the head.

Get a close second shot before trying to convert. If you take a running shot at the head too early and miss inevitably you find yourself in the position of having to try and save shots with your last bowl. Draw close while you still have some artillery left and, having obtained it, you can then go for a conversion shot with more confidence. When playing conversion shots always play them at a pace that, if played correctly, will allow for some margin of error.

Remember – it is not the shot that one plays that brings the results, but the pace at which it is played. Newcomers should steer clear of playing shots with pace until they have mastered the strength of the green.

Always play the correct weight on the 'in-between' shots – the yard-on, firm shot and trail – and make sure that it is the minimum required to do the job. By this I mean that if you want to wrest a jack high bowl and trail the jack a short distance, then a yard of running is all you require. This is a must, for if you should miss your object your shot will go just behind the jack in a good position and still be of some value. Should you be too heavy you could cause a lot of damage, either by taking the jack too far or simply going straight

through the head. CORRECT weight is very important.

You must not be satisfied with just one bowl close to the head, strive for two or even more before deciding on a positional shot. Remember that you should never just try to draw the jack if your opponent has a jack-high bowl. You must play to beat this shot. A bowl that goes narrow to the jack isn't worth anything. With enough weight you will either wrest the jack-high bowl, trail the jack or if you are wider go nicely into the back of the head.

Always make sure that you have a good back position before attempting a block shot, bearing in mind that the former is a much easier shot to play as it often only needs to finish in a certain area to be effective. A block shot requires much more accuracy. It is also wise not to place a block shot too close to the object you want to block (bowl or jack to be protected) for if the blocking bowl is punched through by a drive your opponent's objective may be achieved. Keep it as

Left: My opponent in the 1982 Kodak Masters final at Worthing, John Snell (Australia) seeking instructions from the marker.

Right: The spoils of victory! The magnificent Townsend Thoresen silver salver presented after the Great Britain v World singles internationals at York in 1981.

Singles play

short as possible. I would only ever play this type of shot if it was the only resort left open to me.

Remember that the ditch side of an end rink will often be faster than the inner hand.

Never be short on heavy greens. Short bowls block the head.

A very important point to remember, not only in singles but in the team games as well, is that bowls is about choosing the right shots at a given point in the game. On most ends there will be several options; what you have to weigh up is which shot gives you the greatest chance of success. It will be your assessment of the situation and subsequent play that will determine who wins the game.

Don't allow any hidebound preferences to dominate your game. A too obvious preference for one hand can be an admission of a weakness which a shrewd opponent will soon detect and exploit.

One final point about the singles game. It is a safe bet that at some time or other an opponent will say that he wished he had gone and examined the head – he would certainly have played differently 'if he had known'. Two points – you have the right at any time to go and inspect the head and secondly, if there is a marker, which there should be, you can always ask him what is the state of the head.

To summarise, the foundation of all good bowls play is the draw shot, which creates confidence in building-up a head. Never be content with a shot even if it's a foot from the head – draw still closer and always keep up with your play. It is as well to remember that as much as you would like to, it is doubtful that you will win every end, but if you don't win an end try to keep your opponent down to singles shots where possible.

Remember as well that LUCK plays a much smaller part in singles as there are far fewer bowls in the head than normally.

Never be afraid to go up and examine the head. It's no good saying to yourself 'I'd have played that shot differently if I had known.'

Some points to remember . . .

(1) Remember the draw shot is the basis of the game. Consistency is the key to success – make every bowl count.

(2) Find the reliable hand and stick to it whenever possible. Never fight a bad hand.

(3) Every good singles player is a craftsman when it comes to delivering the jack.

(4) Play it by ear until you have summed up the green and your opponent.

(5) Endeavour to get your first bowl close as it is the most important you will bowl. It is not only the foundation of the end but a confidence booster and will surely pressurise your opponent.

(6) Size up your opponent and try to exploit his weaknesses.
    (a) Does he favour one hand more than the other?
    (b) How good is his drive?
    (c) Does he play it tight?
    (d) What is he like tactically?
    (e) How does he deal with pressure?
    (f) Does he appear relaxed?
    (g) Does he play too many running shots?
    (h) How does the bias on his bowl compare with yours?
    (i) Is his style, stance and delivery suited more to fast or slow greens?
    (j) How experienced is he?

(7) Use the mat and jack to advantage. It is very important to find what suits you or does not suit your opponent and be able to place the mat and deliver the jack in the exact positions.

(8) Do not let your opponent force you off the good hand or the hand you are playing. Make sure you have something close before changing to attempt a different shot. Never try to convert early in an end; instead, play for a good second shot.

(9) Play it tight. If you cannot score settle for second shot. Your opponent cannot go far on singles.

(10) Never vary the length of the jack while you are outbowling your opponent.

(11) Always try to pressurise your opponent. If you have a good lead that is the time to lift your game because he will be trying doubly hard to lift his. Do not be a player who relaxes when in front.

(12) Do not take unnecessary risks. Any risk you take should be a calculated one – e.g. drawing an extra shot to keep the pressure on your opponent when he has back bowls. This should only be done when you have a reasonable lead and a miss at that stage could be disastrous for him.

(13) Remember that the running bowl is more often than not the hardest to play and an objective missed means a bowl out of the head. Size up the situation and the green and decide if it is worth it – you may well be better off settling for the draw or the drive. The pace of the green will have a considerable bearing on your decision.

(14) Before employing the drive look for the worst that can happen – often it does!

(15) If there is a danger learn how to take one or give one.

On the mat against Bob Sutherland in the 1983 Embassy Indoor semi-final. I lost this one 20-21 – but I learned from it!

(16) Make sure you have at least two bowls in the head before worrying about positional bowls.

(17) Only play a block shot as a last resort.

Singles play

(18) Beware of the risks of four close counters against a skilful opponent with the last bowl.

(19) Do not be intimidated by a good driver. Nobody connects all of the time. The fact that he is forced into attacking the head indicates that it is he who is under pressure.

(20) When in trouble think logically and devise a plan for breaking up your opponent's game. Drastic movement of the mat which necessitates a change of line is often very effective but whatever you decide you must believe in and give it your full concentration to capitalise on his mistakes, for he will surely adjust unless you reverse the pressure.

(21) Always appear to your opponent patient, serene, confident, courteous and full of concentration.

(22) Play the game at your pace and do not be over eager to step on to the mat.

(23) Do not underrate your opponent. If you are lying several shots and he has back bowls, place one with them. Play safe – it pays dividends.

(24) Do remember to assess the head as a percentage situation. Ask yourself the following questions:

    (a) What do I stand to gain?
    (b) What do I stand to lose?
    (c) What is the state of the game?
    (d) Is this the time to play it?

(25) Are you a player who easily loses his length after driving? If so drive with discretion and remember to relax sufficiently before playing the next bowl.

(26) Never follow your opponent's line unless you are absolutely certain his bowl is biasing the same as yours. Ninety-nine per cent of the time his bowl and line will differ from your own and the course it takes will only be important if you intend to block with your next delivery.

(27) Analyse your games objectively. Win or lose you can always learn something – this is the way to improve!

(28) Do not nibble at your opponent's bowl if it is close to the jack – draw a close second.

(29) When holding shots do not be afraid of wrecking the head with your last bowl. Stay cool and concentrate on perfect line which ensures that if you are overweight no damage will be done.

(30) Apply the MUST rule for every bowl. I must be up, I must not be narrow, I must get a length etc.

(31) When under great pressure take deep breaths and remember bowls is about three things – PATIENCE, CONCENTRATION and COMMON SENSE.

Above: What a Cliff-hanger! When under pressure against Hartlepool's Cliff Simpson in the 1983 English indoor final I remembered patience, concentration and common sense. It paid off . . . I won 21-20. Right: With Norma Shaw of Durham and England — the 1981 Women's World singles champion.

Teamwork

Teamwork

The vital roles of lead, No.2, No.3 and skip

The vast majority of bowls games played in the UK will consist of team games – whether it is for three players (triples) or four (rinks).

The simplest form of bowls is of course between two players, singles, and you also get many competitions that feature two players, a lead and skip, who play as a pairs team.

But most matches at club, county and international level will be between teams of four – the lead, No. 2, No. 3 and a skip. In the Federation code of bowls they do not have fours but feature three players, a lead, No. 2 and skip.

In the last chapter I dealt with play in singles. This time I will analyse the role of each player in the fours team beginning of course with the LEAD.

After the two skips have tossed a coin to determine the order of play and the winning skip has decided to deliver the jack first, his lead will then be required to place the mat. The laws of the game are quite clear on the procedure here – the front edge of the mat should be placed six feet from the front edge of the ditch with the centre of the mat along the centre line of the rink.

The mat can be centred by use of the centre rink marker on the bank. The skip at the other end will also help to ensure that the mat is correctly positioned.

The lead will then roll the jack to a position which will be determined by the skip. He may ask his lead to play a specific length, or give him the choice of determining the length.

Whichever, it is important to remember that the lead, like all members of the team, is under the direction of his skip at all times.

The lead, once the jack has been correctly positioned, will then deliver his bowl giving possession of the rink to his opposing lead once his bowl has come to rest.

From then on all players will bowl alternately.

It is most important for a lead to be able to draw competently to the jack. The most satisfying shot in the game of bowls is still the draw and no one in bowls gets a better chance to execute this shot than a lead. So a good lead will always try to draw that first bowl as close to the jack as possible.

Too many leads, when they find that their opposing lead has drawn a good shot close to the jack, either try changing their hand or put a heavier bowl into the head in the hope of disturbing other bowls or the jack.

This is fatal – a lead should always try to bowl the good hand on the rink. If his opposing lead has done this and placed a bowl fairly close to the draw, even if it is in the draw, he should still play that hand striving to draw as close to the jack as possible. He should ignore the short bowl in the knowledge that if he makes contact he will probably play it into a jack high position.

It will then give him, if it was a first bowl, a chance to draw with his second bowl or give the No. 2 a chance to play a draw shot.

Having drawn a close shot with his first bowl, even a 'toucher' (a bowl which during its travel on the green has touched the jack is marked with a piece of chalk and remains a 'live' bowl as long as it remains within the confines of the rink), the lead should then be thinking of drawing another shot,

Harmony in a rink is so important and David Bryant found it with this quartet which helped England to the 1983 British championships. Back row: Left – Gerry Smyth (lead, Paddington), right – Andy Thomson (No. 3 Cyphers). Front: David Bryant (skip, Clevedon), David Rhys-Jones (No. 2, Clevedon).

preferably behind the jack.

I suggest this, because there is always the danger when a lead plays two bowls very close to the jack of offering the opposing team a bigger target to go for. And it is a well-known fact that nine times out of ten if a jack is moved it goes to the back of the rink.

So a good lead will always try to place a second bowl, if he has succeeded in drawing his first, to a good position. He should not try to broaden the head.

Teams who can boast a good lead have a big advantage over others because the lead is the man who lays the foundation stones for a good head. It is perhaps a pity that so many players, once they have established themselves as a lead, then want to move on from that position to play elsewhere in the team.

One point a lead must always remember is that individual success counts less than the victory of the team. Often in a match it becomes a battle between the two leads. While this is of course good in providing a competitive edge to the game, it must not be at the expense of the other players.

I have always held some fairly strong views about leads – some of which haven't necessarily conformed with what certain authorities and writers would naturally agree.

So far as I am concerned the shot doesn't really matter. I wouldn't be upset if my lead failed to give me a shot in several ends. What I do want from him is two useful bowls – two bowls right in the head that can be used for promoting, resting, running through and so on – always assuming that the jack isn't moved to some remote part of the rink.

I do not expect my leads to alter the mat or jack position unless I specifically request it. Altering the length of the jack in terms of yards is difficult enough, but if you couple this this different green as well life would be even more difficult.

My lead must do everything in his power to maintain the same conditions that are proving most successful to the team.

Teamwork

If the opposing four are proving more accurate as a group, then mat changes are not only inevitable but an essential to disrupt their play.

One other point that annoys me is when an opposing lead gets one shot on the jack and my lead then forgets all the ground rules and immediately tries to knock him off, instead of bowling as close to the jack as he can. A lead must accept that his opponent's bowl is a good one and try to draw alongside it or to it. He should try to broaden the head to provide an easier target for his second man.

Always be wary of playing a shot where failure does not justify the risk.

So if I was laying down some ground rules for leads they would be:-

(1) Use the mat correctly and to the advantage of your team. Don't fiddle about with the mat just for the sake of it.

(2) Make good use of the jack and if the skip dictates a certain length make sure that you reach it. And remember to roll the jack properly – don't sling it. Careless rolling can be fatal.

(3) Decide which is the best hand for bowling and stick to it. Play up and down the same side where possible.

(4) DON'T change your hand just because the opposition bowl appears to be in the way. Ignore it and draw to the jack. You will often get the shot or even a good second.

(5) Always try to get your bowls near to the jack but bear in mind that it is often better to have a second bowl just behind the jack, keeping the target area narrow.

(6) DON'T be short when shot is against you. It is better to have a bowl a yard through the head than a similar distance in front.

(7) AVOID taking too narrow a line to the jack. It is better if anything to be too wide. And avoid leaving jack high bowls.

No club bowler has ever reached top class without mastering good length draw bowling and this is an essential quality for a lead. It also provides the essentials that must be ground into a bowler if he hopes to emulate his more experienced colleagues in top competitions.

In many ways the No. 2 is complementary to the lead and as such his task is simply to rectify what the lead may have failed to achieve or to balance and improve a promising position.

Whatever the No. 2 has to do, this position is thought by many to be one of the most difficult to fill despite the fact that many club selectors seem to think that it is an ideal place to stick the beginners.

I believe this is a very false idea of the importance of the No. 2 and probably grew out of the fact that when many club teams are picked they usually decide to put the best bowlers in the No. 3 or skip positions and any specialist leads obviously pick themselves, leaving the least experienced players for the No. 2 spots.

So a false idea of the importance of the No. 2 slowly grew.

In fact his difficulties may increase if his lead is playing very well! This might sound odd but if his lead is doing his stuff then the No.2 will be playing to consolidate and that means bowling to blank positions.

And believe me, trying to put a bowl on a spot devoid of a target or guide is very difficult.

If his lead has failed to get close to the jack then he will be required to put his first bowl into the head, so he will have to be particularly careful about length. In some cases it would be better for him to be slightly short than heavy, so as not to give his No. 3 a more difficult task.

This means that a No. 2 must be good at sizing up the swing of the green.

The No. 2 has to be a very good drawing player and primarily a good length player. He must also be able to play a fast bowl if needed. The lead has an exact shot to play, but with the No. 2 it often doesn't matter, although you want him to be there or very close.

If you have a lead who is a very good close drawing bowler, a No. 2 who is a consistent draw bowler and steady as a rock, then add a No. 3 who perhaps isn't quite as consistent but more versatile, then you have a good basis for a top class rink.

If the shots lie with his side the No. 2 will add to them, protect them or add to the general all-round insurance of the head.

If it was my task to field a strong team I would play my best two length bowlers at lead and No. 2. The No. 2 must be a good draw bowler. It is a prime requirement for this position and he must be able to draw under pressure, because he is the last person who can be guaranteed an open draw at the jack.

By the time the No. 2s have finished often the No. 3 can't get into the head and has to resort to heavy bowls. So if the No. 2 is off that day, you could be in for a very bad time.

Most No. 2s graduate to that position after a period as a lead so should have developed some kind of accuracy in drawing to the jack. He can now be expected to expand his experience and add more to his repertoire of shots. There is no harm in the No. 2 playing running shots as quite often, if they miss the target, they will still land up behind the head and in a useable position.

Play in fours necessitates good teamwork and I see no reason why a No. 2 should not ask questions of his skip and discuss quietly at the end of the rink what tactics to employ and suggest what shots he favours in a particular situation.

I well remember when I was playing No. 2 in the 1962 Commonwealth and Empire Games in Perth, Australia, with Tom Fleming as lead, Les Watson as No. 3 and Sid Drysdale as skip.

Tom and I did chat to Les once or twice and offered our advice on a particular situation. But having offered it we retired quickly from the head so he could continue to ponder without distraction on what advice to offer Sid.

What players can do to help each other most is to encourage whoever is at the other end bowling – be ready with the praise and indeed the sympathy when things don't go quite to plan.

As a No. 2, particularly in those games, I paid very special attention to the greening of my bowls because I considered that if they were greened accurately they were potentially useful, whether they were a little long or a little short, and less likely to do any damage when the position was favourable.

If the shot is against him the No. 2 is usually asked to play a specific shot. When it is not, his task is to put down two useful bowls – remembering that only on the rarest occasions are bowls wide or narrow of the jack or head useful.

To sum up:

● A useful second must be versatile on the green, possessing every shot in the book.

● A second will have the responsibility, vital to his team's chances during an end, of playing whatever shot his skip thinks necessary to either re-establish the head and gain shot or to consolidate a good position.

● The second should always go on to the mat with his mind entirely open as far as what shot should be played.

Teamwork at its best. . .the Middleton inter-county cup final at Worthing. Watched by an enthralled crowd this was in 1981 between Bryant's home county of Somerset (the eventual winners) and Norfolk.

● The No. 2 is the player responsible for keeping the scorecard and scoreboard up to date. He should not only ensure that his card is correct but that it tallies with his opponents'.

● Top class No.2s are invariably very good singles players as they are very consistent and are not put off by mat movement and sudden changes of length of jack.

● Many authorities in the game consider the second man to be the mainstay of the four as often he is the last player to have an open draw to the jack. If he is clearly outbowled by his opposite number life can be very difficult for the team.

The responsibilities of a bowler greatly increase when he takes No.3 spot on the rink. He will obviously be a more experienced player who has graduated through the lead and No.2 positions and will now be versed in the art of the tactics involved with the building up of the head.

The ideal No.3 has to be capable of a variety of shots. He will be asked, perhaps more than any other player, to play such shots as the block, a position bowl and to play a jack trailing

shot. These shots are never easy so the No.3 must be a good 'weight' player.

Most skips prefer a No.3 who can play forcing shots if required but even the most enthusiastic No.3 should know how to use these shots with discretion.

The player at No.3 is the skip's right-hand man – second in command. He must point out everything to the skip to make sure that he hasn't missed anything. He must pose the questions. Although I personally also like to bring my lead and No.2 into a discussion of tactics, the No.3 is the man who is entitled to put forward his opinions to the skip.

Often when a No.2 graduates to a more permanent No.3 spot he feels it necessary to advise the skip on every move. It's probably because as a No.2 he had lots of ideas but had to keep them bottled-up and now that his chance has arisen feels he can at last put those theories into practice. He might also find himself playing with a skip who isn't quite as good as the skip he played with previously as a No.2 – so he will be hard pushed to stay tight-lipped.

Teamwork

So there is one point a No.3 must guard against. It is amazing how often I have seen a No.3 leap in with his suggestion for a shot just as the skip is about to send down his first bowl – often with disastrous results.

Quite often the skip has in fact thought of the No.3's alternative and rejected it in his mind as not the best shot to play in the circumstances. It is important to remember that the skip is in charge of the rink and must be firmly backed on whatever shot he produces.

The successful No.3 watches every shot that is sent down. His first duty is to collaborate and get in tune with his skip. It is important that they have a good understanding.

One of the first things a No.3 should remember is never to condemn the opinion of his skip on a particular shot he has requested. The shot may appear impossible from the mat, but on crossing over the picture may become clearer.

So to all new, and for that matter experienced thirds as well, I would say always play your shots with loyalty or the half-hearted shot that you subsequently produce will be regretted when you reach the other end.

A successful No.3 should have a good temperament, and will have to get on with the other players. He must be capable of helping and encouraging the lead and No.2, making sure that they maintain their confidence and concentration.

I often hear a lot of silly things said in bowls – like the remark that the skip has two bowls, one his own and the other his No.3's. That's silly as the skip has to make the final decision and bowl both his two bowls.

If one bowl was his third's he probably wouldn't be able to play the shot he wanted. It may take him one shot to open the head and the other to draw shot.

In most competitive games of bowls the No.3 and the skip will be together at the head so they will be working side-by-side in building it. This is very important in creating a good understanding.

I like a third who has a bit of flair; a player capable of playing all the shots; one who is enthusiastic and can be heard. You don't want an out-and-out introvert as a No.3. He must be able to generate excitement among the other players. If you look at international level, the ones who are most successful are those that you know are out there on the green. Invariably they seem to get the best results.

A No.3 must always take care when replying to the skip's request for instructions on the position of the head. It will rankle a skip if he is given incorrect information.

Sometimes he will ask what effect an opponent's bowl has had on the head. Here a No.3 must be clear with his reply and take all things into consideration.

Too often a No.3 will simply say – 'We're two up, just draw another' – while ignoring the fact that the opposition have two good back bowls. The trail shot might be difficult, but you must never underestimate the skill of the opposition. In these circumstances it might have been better to ask for some cover at the back of the head to take away the danger.

A No.3 must always be positive when asked by his skip who is holding shot. It won't be of much benefit to a skip to be told that he is holding shot and then, after playing a safety shot, he finds out that he was in fact one down – especially if he wanted to trail the jack a few inches for two shots but paired something else instead!

The last shot that a skip plays can invariably be a vital one. So the conditions under which he executes the shot must be the

Would the players move, please, we can't see! Fascinated spectators watching Bryant's Somerset rink in action.

best. The third should not distract him from his efforts.

If a No.3 has any suggestions to make to his skip, these should be at the head. A skip doesn't want any instructions when he's on the mat preparing to play a particular shot. This is the wrong time for a No.3 to give further advice.

In some respects the job of a third will seem more difficult to that of the skip as he is often asked to play some fairly impossible looking shots. But it is often better for the third to patch up any lapse by the other members of the team than leave it all to the skip.

The effective third also gives nothing away when measuring. The shot must be doubtful for him to ask for a measure in the first place, so he must never be 'bluffed' out of going for the tapes. When a No.3 has dealt with the obvious shots he should always look around for those to be gained further from a measure. The No.3 will also be expected to mark a skip's 'touchers' and remove 'dead' bowls to the bank.

I have been fortunate to have played with some really good No.3s like David Rhys-Jones and Ted Hayward. A good No.3 is invaluable to the rink.

Some people would say that the skip's position is the most difficult and most important on the rink. Some would say that the skip has to be the best player on the rink. Certainly he will have to be a very good player, but the most important task will be to establish his team as a unit and get the best out of the other three players with him.

The skip of a four has far more to do than just play his two bowls.

Briefly a skip will have to do all of the following things:-
   (1) Study the green and the playing conditions.
   (2) Watch every move on the green.
   (3) Sum up his opponents.
   (4) Sort out his opponents' strengths and weaknesses.
   (5) Know the strengths and weaknesses of his own team.
   (6) Inspire his own players to bring out their best.
   (7) Give full encouragement to players both when they are playing well and particularly lifting them when they are playing badly.
   (8) Give clear instructions on what shot he wants.
   (9) Bring all players into discussions of tactics.
   (10) Produce every shot in the book to inspire by example.

These are just some of the things a good skip will need to do. So you can see the massive responsibility that this position carries. It is the ability of a skip to inspire his rink that can make all the difference. He must be a first-class diplomat with a very even temperament. He must create harmony within his rink, make the players feel that they are part of his team and always remain serene under pressure.

The skip's ability to play under pressure is vital. If he can remain calm and pull-off some good shots when shots down, he will ultimately take the pressure off his own players and help to lift their game.

In a similar vein he must also keep the opposition guessing. He must never appear to be in trouble, even if the odds are heavily stacked against him.

The skip must also be a master tactician. Tactics will play a big part in his game so he must have firm knowledge of his craft and the ability to carry it out. He must have the ability to be able to 'read' the head to see where he needs to place his team's shots, while also making it more difficult for his opponents to succeed, and re-establishing his team's control when the opposition have taken the shot.

Control of his rink is important. He must never ask a player to play a shot he knows that he isn't capable of, and have enough commonsense to help one of his players who is having difficulty in mastering a particular hand or shot.

In this type of situation it may be that he needs to get this player playing the draw shot on one hand for a few ends until he has got his confidence back. The skip must also remember that what might suit him doesn't necessarily suit all his players.

The skip has to be switched-on for the full duration of a game. He can't afford to miss a trick; there is always something to occupy his mind.

A danger can be that the skip will pour himself so much into helping his team-mates that his own game may get neglected. A skip bowls every shot on the green, both his own team's and his opponents'.

It is very important for a skip to give his players sound directions.

It's no good just saying 'I want one around here'. He must be positive, say as few words as possible, but make those words count. He must indicate the pace required for certain shots and be precise on where he wants a positional bowl played.

He should know something about the type of bowls his players are using, not just so that he can identify them in the head, but also to know whether they take a narrow or wide line to the jack.

If he has a left-handed player in his rink he should realise that they will take a different line to the jack, so he can take advantage of this and get this player to play shots that the others perhaps can't.

In short, he must exploit the strengths of his own players and the weaknesses of his opponents.

A common fault of some skips is to feel that they must

Bryant and his Somerset colleague Jim O'Brien (No. 3) consider the next move, during an England match.

Teamwork

always hold shot each end, no matter what. Seeing their opponents' bowl nearest to the jack is like a red rag to a bull – they've got to knock it off. Many big losses can be prevented by getting a good second rather than attempting a wild drive. Alternatively, it is sometimes equally as dangerous to pack the head too early, thus presenting a big target.

A skip should never get complacent, particularly if his team is doing really well. There is often a danger around the 17th and 18th ends of slackening off if well in front, which could be fatal if your opponents suddenly hit a good patch. Remember that a big lead can just as easily disappear as be gained.

It is easier to play at your best when the odds are in your favour. A good skip asserts himself when the odds are against.

It is difficult for ambitious bowlers to resist the pressure of taking on the skip's role. Indeed many see it as an accolade to their improved bowling skills, but it is sometimes a danger for younger players to be given the responsiblity of a rink too early. It would be better for them to play No.3 in a top-class rink than to be given the skip's role in a poor rink.

As has already been said, a successful team is a unit. Therefore, the greater the understanding between the players the more capably they will perform under extreme pressure. Post-mortems can be invaluable if conducted in the correct manner. If a game is analysed constructively with the view of improving the performance, all bowlers should never lose sight of the fact that however good they are, or think they are, the game of bowls is such that one never stops learning.

However, such discussions should be confined to the immediate team and should take place off the green and never on it. I strongly believe a first class skip should only encourage and never criticise and if he hasn't anything good to say he should keep quiet. It is this message that he has to convey to the fellow members of his four as it is equally important that they should adopt the same attitude to their skip, who, when facing situations of extreme pressure will be more likely to perform creditably knowing he has the full backing of his colleagues.

Four players, playing as a unit with the knowledge that there will never be any dissent on the rink can, in my opinion, benefit from tactical discussions off the green. Obviously no four bowlers will always read the head the same way and good natured criticism off the green on the tactics employed during the match often leads for a better understanding of the game by all concerned and in turn strengthens the team's loyalty to one another.

It has sometimes been suggested that a skip will play the later stages of the head so as to leave himself the most spectacular shot on which to finish. If he does this, and I don't believe that there are many who would, then he's not a good skip.

The ideal skip is not only courteous and tactful but will also have the ability to arouse and sustain the interests of his players keeping them enthusiastic and happy while giving them the feeling that they are playing with him and not so much for him. In short the ideal skip is a leader.

As in this English Women's fours final at Leamington in 1981, the job of the No.3 is to advise the skip of the shots for or against, while the lead (left) prepared for the next end and the No.2 (second left) notes the score.

EXPERIENCE

Knowledge of playing surfaces

Varieties of greens and their effect

It's important to have a knowledge of playing surfaces in order to assess how to tackle them.

Cumberland turf greens were always considered the ultimate in grass bowling surfaces. It is a very fine rounded blade grass which is ideal for playing bowls on because it keeps its levels and has fast-drying qualities, draining well. You can also roll the surface and because it is on sand it doesn't compact.

The quality of greens is always allied to greenkeeping. In the old days, when there were some marvellous greenkeepers, and the knowledge was handed down from father to son, they really used to go for Cumberland-turf greens. The trouble is that it is not a very deep-rooted grass and it can't stand droughts and therefore has to be watered regularly.

One of the best greens that I ever played bowls on was at Mortlake, where they used to hold the national championships before moving to Worthing. That was a Cumberland-turf green.

In the past emphasis was placed on preparing a playing surface and free-running green on which the player could display all his skills and attempt a full range of shots. Unfortunately today the emphasis has changed and it is now placed on retaining healthy turf at the expense of the playing surface – little better than a superb lawn.

The true comparison, I suppose is a cricketer batting on a good wicket which is hard and true, as opposed to facing a bowler on a bumpy green strip where the ball could go anywhere.

I mention the cricket square because the requirements of a good cricket wicket are similar to that of a bowling green although not of course to the same degree. In both cases it is essential that they be free of bumps and have a smooth, firm, evenly covered surface. I appreciate that the degree of compaction that takes place on a cricket wicket cannot apply to a bowling green, but a certain amount of rolling is necessary to achieve a good playing surface.

Immediately after the second world war, when I joined the Clevedon Bowling Club most of the clubs in our area employed their own full-time greenkeepers. But gradually, in the ensuing years as costs increased, more and more clubs had to dispense with their services. The days have now gone when the greenkeeper used to hollow-tyne a 40 yard square green by hand and water the green late at night, again by hand, in order to prevent it burning up!

One of the problems that faced Cumberland turf was that taken out of its natural environment it tended to get other grasses seeding into it and you ended up with a '57' varieties. These were free-running greens but these days the tendency to use a mixture of sand/soil and peat as a top dressing has tended to slow down green speeds when the proportion of peat is excessive.

Also, with the use of grass mixtures which are of a courser variety, a green is produced with a lot more friction which is heavier. The main reason, however, these days for heavier greens is that they are not cut as regularly or closely as they should be. This makes the green moist and it doesn't dry out properly.

I also firmly believe that greens are not rolled enough and this, allied to the longer length of grass, makes them slower. The more grass that you leave on a green, the more you will get 'tracking'.

A good knowledge of playing surfaces can be invaluable to a player. If you know what it takes to create a good bowling surface you will be able to use that knowledge to your advantage.

As I stated before, Cumberland turf greens have always been considered the ultimate in grass bowling surfaces. Enlightened bowling green contractors lay Cumberland turf on a bed of sand, or a mixture containing a very high percentage of sand, and as subsequent dressings are of a similar content, the surface can be rolled fairly regularly without too much fear of compaction.

It is useful for a bowler when he goes to play on a green that he takes a good look to sort out in his mind its characteristics and know the type of game he is going to have to play.

He must remember that the pace of the green is not only determined by the closeness of the cut, or by the rolling, but by how clean the grass is. If a grass is not looked after you get a build-up of thatch which gives a spongy effect to the green that results in peculiar runs. And the less it is cut, the more thatch you will get.

A good playing surface on the day requires good greenkeeping and good equipment. Two examples above are the Scott Bonnar mower and Worthing 'rink master' Jock Munro (second from left).

It is essential, therefore, that a green is cut regularly, ideally not less than three times a week as this prevents the grass from getting coarse and encourages bushy growth. This not only applies to the playing season as during the Autumn and Spring reasonable growth can be expected and, if neglected, the finely-bladed even textured surface can revert to a rougher mixture containing numerous coarse stalks.

In the southern hemisphere most greens are rolled several times in a week whereas in this country there is a school of thought which believes that the weight of the roller on the mower is sufficient to provide a good playing surface.

I, like many others, cannot go along with this as all the best greens I have ever played on have, at regular intervals throughout the season, been subjected to some form of rolling. And I firmly believe that after Autumn tyning and heavy slitting etc, which opens up the playing surface, rolling is particularly necessary at the beginning of the season.

Unfortunately, the majority of greenkeepers, who feel that the weight of the roller on the mower is sufficient to polish the playing surface and roll the soil immediately below the grass, do not cut their greens close enough to allow the roller to have sufficient effect. Invariably there is a built-up of thatch when close mowing does not take place and the mower's roller rides over this cushion which prevents any ironing out of irregularities in the soil structure immediately below.

There is no doubt that rolling does cause compaction and any experienced first-class greenkeeper who really knows his job, spikes and slits regularly throughout the playing season to keep his green aerated. This treatment, combined with tyning in the Autumn, more than adequately deals with any ill-effects that rolling may have on the playing area.

Regular scarifying and the use of the comb on the mower provides a clean green which enables a light roller to be used to maximum effect during the playing season which in turn ensures that the bowler enjoys a free-running and regular surface.

Most of the greens in the UK are put down with turf, although there is much to be said for seeding a green. Other countries have different approaches to laying greens.

In South Africa, where labour costs are cheaper than in the UK, they plant each piece of grass at equal distances which then creeps and covers with regular watering.

In Australia they do seed greens but also take the tops off their greens and lay them elsewhere. Australian greens are mainly 'bent' or 'couch' grasses. Both grasses by our standards have deep-rooting qualities. Because of our type of weather, our grasses don't have to go so far down into the soil to search for moisture as those in Australia.

Couch grass is particularly deep-rooting, even more than bent. The couch is a coarser grass which must be cut tightly. The tift-dwarf greens, like those at the 1982 Commonwealth Games at the Moorooka Club, is an American grass with a creeping habit and as its growth is mainly horizontal, the vertical growth is as slow as its name implies.

Australian greenkeepers are meticulous in the way that they cut their greens – cutting and rolling regularly. They suffer compaction in the same way that we do, but this can be remedied.

Compaction, the cause of many problems on a bowls green, seems to be a dirty word with some turf research establishments. If you get compaction you can expect the grass not to grow so well and bald patches to appear. But, of course, this

Knowledge of playing surfaces

David Bryant inspects a Cameron pop-up sprinkler system which can be programmed to water at night when maximum results are achieved.

will happen if it isn't treated correctly!

Rolling can give compaction, but spiking will give the green air. So it's obvious that you need to tyne after you have rolled.

When you think we only play on our outdoor greens for about five months in the year, it is quite easy to tyne a green regularly in the Autumn. This will break up the surface and let the air in ready for the beginning of the season the following year when the green should then be rolled.

Australian and New Zealand players are amazed when they come over to the UK to find out how little we cut and roll our greens. They are often told – 'well we have a different climate over here! – but after all, all you need to make grass grow is sunshine and water.

We get plenty of water and a reasonable amount of sunshine. We may not get quite the amount of sunshine as they do in Australia, but being too hot can be detrimental. So I think, in the main, our climate is quite suitable for grass growing. After all, we can grow a wide variety of fruit and vegetables and overseas visitors, particularly those from 'down under', are always impressed by the vividness of our greenery.

I also think it very surprising that some people believe you can't produce good greens in Scotland. OK, they may be a little behind at the start of the season, but within a couple of weeks they've caught up. It's never quite as hot up there, but that doesn't matter too much.

Their greens are slower simply because they will not cut them down properly, or often enough, or use a roller.

Most greens that I have played on north of the border tend to be very heavy and of poor quality. As there are good greens

in Bournemouth and in Bristol which are in different locations, it can't be the fact that the climate is different.

Bowls has made great strides in recent years in selling itself as a sport but I firmly believe that it's not much good having top competitions, television coverage and sponsors coming in, if you haven't got any decent greens to play on. Maintenance of a bowling green is therefore very important.

When a bowler goes along to a club he can pretty well assess how the greens going to play by looking at the texture of the grass and by looking to see if the surface looks polished or bumpy. He then has to adopt his play to the conditions.

It therefore follows that it is more difficult for a player who comes off a really good green to go and play on a really bad one, than the other way round. The player who plays on a bad green has to concentrate so much on getting his line right, because he knows that if he is a fraction out he is going to go off at a tangent, but on a good green he finds it that much easier.

Bad greens are also usually heavier. If you get on a nice, easy paced, reliable green you can play bowls. If you play on a heavy, bumpy green I think that you have to forget about the finer arts, make up your mind right from the start that there is nothing for short-ones, make sure you get more bowls in the head than your opponent and tend to play attacking bowls.

A bad green brings everyone to the same level.

In the southern hemisphere they have very fast greens of different grasses which are very well cut and rolled. They also have much bigger clubs, many with more than one green, which means they have more money available to employ greenkeepers.

The Australians have also perfected some of the best

machinery for looking after bowling greens – mechanised mowers, tyning machines, rollers etc.

Many greens in the UK are badly out on levels and, basically, the only way to level them is to fill in the hollows. The Australian greens are more or less dead level. In order to keep them this way they put their dressing on so as to leave an identical amount everywhere. When we dress our greens we tend to broadcast it and brush it out reasonably evenly which, of course, never quite works out.

Anyone who plays bowls and wants to play the game seriously – to become an expert at the game – must think deeply about the game in every respect. That's why it is important that the greenkeeper is a bowls player as well.

There are many greenkeepers who can keep a first-class piece of grass, but they don't honestly know what bowlers really want. Having looked at greens throughout the world and talked to the people who look after them, I can appreciate what goes into the production of a first-class bowling green.

Most greens in the UK are put down with turf, which is either bedded in on a sand base, which is the best because sand finds its own levels, or a soil mixture. One of the most important aspects after a green has been laid, and indeed in any long-standing green, is a good watering system.

If the watering system is wrong then the green isn't going to be so healthy. The ideal watering system is one that gives you an even distribution in as short a time as possible. The best system I know is a pop-up sprinkler system all the way round the green. While it may be expensive to fit initially it proves cost effective because it doesn't require much maintenance and waters quickly at the throw of a switch.

Correct watering is essential. Over-watering is worse than under-watering and applying it at night time is also very important. The pop-up sprinkler system can be programmed to water at night when maximum results can be achieved without soaking the green too heavily. When the greenkeeper arrives in the morning he usually finds the grass dry and ideal for cutting. It must always be remembered that only sufficient water to keep the grass green is required. Excess watering makes the green soft and heavy and therefore more easily damaged. A firm surface plays better and wears well, providing it is healthy.

There is also much to be said for seeding the green and having a watering system built-in at the same time. It is much easier to lay a level green with seed than with turf and once your seed has germinated you can keep it watered with the system, which will help to keep it growing steadily.

And, as with any green, you must keep screeding regularly as it grows to get a nice smooth surface. You can, of course, add additional seed in the screed and in a short space of time achieve a billiard-like top.

Average pace of a green in the British Isles is between 10/11 seconds – not very fast.

In New Zealand they play on a weed – cotula (swamp weed) – which looks a bit like the duck weed which floats on ponds in the UK, although it differes by having a leaf with a serrated-edge and spreads on runners. This is a great surface to play bowls on and is easily kept level. You can actually bury it and the leaf will still come through as the runners spread under the surface. It will also stand close cutting and is very adaptable to rolling, standing any amount of compaction.

Funnily enough it runs better in damp conditions than when the sun is shining. In sunshine the leaf of the weed tends to curl

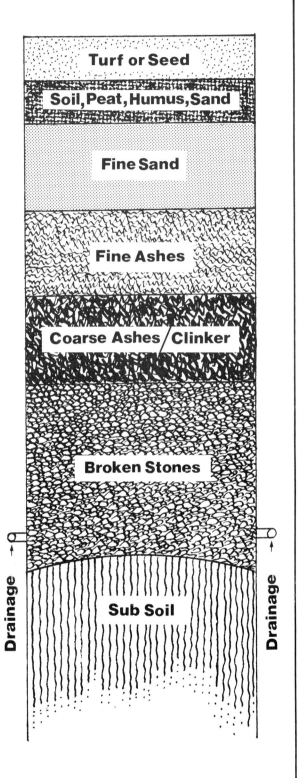

Structure of a typical UK outdoor green illustrating the various layers which go into providing a sound base at the same time allowing good drainage and favourable growing conditions. Depth of soil depends on whether the green is to be turfed or seeded.

Knowledge of playing surfaces

which gives more friction to the bowls surface, while in damp conditions it lies flat cutting down on the friction. It can also stand severe winter conditions – but not excess heat. It must never be watered artificially in sunshine as this will cause scorching to the surface.

A most interesting facet of this surface is the way it's propagated. We scarify a green to clear thatch and to let air into the playing surface, but the cotula surface is scarified by biting into the soil to a certain depth and this is a form of root-pruning. As you do this, you tear the runners and they come out into the air. Then you go over the green with a mower to collect the cuttings and a new green can be laid with these scarifications.

If it's a grass green, you can scarify the grass by biting into the soil sufficiently deep to leave a groove into which can be swept all the prunings from your cotula green. All that is then required is to top dress, water, and the cotula will grow and eventually take over from the grass. The original green, which was scarified and root-pruned, is top dressed and where the pruning has taken place the air stimulates fresh growth. It proves very economical because you are helping to keep two greens in fettle. The cotula scarifications can also be used for repair work.

My experiences of cotula greens have taught me that they fall into two categories – green cotula and brown. It's the same weed but with the brown cotula the warmer it gets the faster it becomes. The green cotula is definitely more succulent and gives more grip.

My only criticism with cotula greens is that they can be too fast. New Zealand, which is the only country with this surface, has put more emphasis on speed, therefore their play is very much a draw and drive game. The average pace is round about the 19 second-mark, too fast for all-round play. Many reach speeds in excess of this. It makes our 'yard-on' shot impossible.

There are now moves in New Zealand to slow these greens down. Australian greens are about the right speeds in the main, whereas we need to improve our speeds and the standard. South African greens tend to be a little bumpy because they don't roll. I have played on greens in Canada which tend to be very heavy, but I don't know an awful lot about the greens in America, although I believe that the west coast ones are quite good.

Having discussed grass surfaces I now want to move onto synthetics.

Personally I can't really see the synthetic surface taking off because there are two problems. First is drainage. If you are going to have a successful green of any type you must have good drainage. It's not good water draining away in one spot and not another.

You actually get this on some grass bowling greens – hard dry spots which always tend to pick up speed. So therefore, with a synthetic green, you must have even drainage and while there are various systems that partly achieve this they haven't really been successful. I consider we achieved this at Sole Bay where we could get the water away very well, but there are other problems.

You then have to find a successful carpet to go on the top and invariably you require an underlay with it that will give the correct speed. It may be possible eventually to produce a carpet without an underlay, but it hasn't been done yet.

You have to produce a surface where the bowl will bite and behave consistently. The experience I have had so far with

synthetic surfaces is that they are badly affected by wind. While this is perfectly acceptable in Australia and New Zealand on their fast surfaces, the average bowler in the British Isles is not happy to see his bowl suddenly career wildly across the green when a gust of wind takes it.

That isn't the only problem. When you play on grass all day you suddenly become aware that the green is tracking badly and becomes difficult to bowl. However, when you come the following day and the greens have been cut it will be back to normal. The grass has recovered and is standing up again. But this cannot happen with an artificial carpet. The more you play on it – the more it is going to track and will therefore become more and more difficult to bowl.

There is really no substitute for something that is growing that will replace itself.

You can argue that you have this problem indoors as well but what you don't experience indoors is the effect of the wind. So I can't ever see synthetic surfaces taking the place of

grass, although it's a substitute that is obviously better than nothing.

I have always held some fairly strong views on indoor surfaces. I think there are many mistakes made with the selection of materials for the indoor game. Obviously the first thing to consider in building an indoor green, excluding the actual building itself, is the screed. Any club putting down an indoor green must be certain of getting the screed right. Many are very difficult to play because they have a surface under the carpet that was badly screeded. Bowling then becomes a lottery.

I have had considerable personal experience of laying indoor carpets over the last 10 years and I know some of the problems. What must be realised right away is that what's acceptable as a screed for ordinary buildings isn't good enough for bowling. So you need to employ an expert at this particular job.

The least important item in my mind is the actual playing

Secret of a good indoor green is first a perfect screed and secondly the right type of underlay which determines pace and performance. Many mistakes are made in selection of materials which can make bowling something of a lottery.

surface – the carpet. What is more important is the underlay. Underlay determines the pace and also the performance – what the bowl does.

You have to remember when choosing an underlay that after a while this will compress with the amount of wear and this could change the pace over its lifecycle. It might have a certain swing when first laid, but this will alter as it wears. The green will become faster and the swing more exaggerated. So selecting an underlay is very important.

I could never recommend a hair type underlay or one of the artificial fibres as, although initially they play well, uneven compression becomes more and more evident as the years pass which makes the green increasingly more difficult for both line and length. The rinks tend to play like a grassy outdoor green which is tracking badly in as much that it seems impossible to find the middle of the rink. And when one goes outside a line the bowl not only hangs but drops short as it is travelling over softer underlay. Conversely, when narrow, the bowl appears to pick up speed as it crosses the middle of the rink where compression is at its greatest.

In my opinion, the best type of underlay is rubber. A suitable rubber or crumb-rubber underlay (or foam) will last for a number of years. Crumb-rubber may tend to get slower as it wears, because it gets softer but it is resilient and springs back so that it does not compress. It maintains an even pace across the green and minimises tracking. The speed will only vary with temperature and humidity.

You get the odd little trick creeping into indoor surfaces, especially where the carpet wears more in one spot than another.

There are quite a number of carpets to choose from; some are better than others. I think that you have to look at them all to make your selection. Some carpets are 'elastic' and need stretching regularly while others don't. You have to consider the 'wear' factor and what happens while it wears. Some perform better as they get older – like 'Greengauge' – others, as they get thinner, produce tricks.

I have often thought that a carpet with an integral backing would have some advantages over the established method of separate surface and underlay. Backed carpets are available but recommended for use only as a 'roll up' surface. Recently, however, a new carpet called Greentex came on to the market. It has a needle punched surface, integral rubber backing and is for use on permanent greens.

The advantages of this type of carpet are: Reduced laying costs; low maintenance costs – no stretching required; no rucking of underlay and carpet; players can move more freely on the green without fear of damaging the carpets; tracking is greatly reduced; a consistant speed is maintained across the green due to even tension; the playing surface is completely free of bumps etc.

To summarise:
(1) Screed very important – if wrong, replace.
    Underlays very important to determine both pace and performance.
(3) Get hold of the experts to advise and deal with the above.
(4) Get the right combination of carpet and underlay.
(5) Get the right combination of carpet and underlay to suit the width of rinks.
(6) A carpet with an integral backing is the most reliable and requires the least maintenance.

Adapting to playing conditions

How to adapt grip, stance and delivery

There are a wide variety of playing conditions in any one country, let alone throughout the world. So it means that there are quite a number of decisions to be made before you get on the green to bowl.

First of all you will have to decide how to adapt your grip, stance and delivery. The choice of what bowl to use is also going to have a major effect. And lastly, you will have to select the right type of game to play to suit the conditions.

In the first part of the section on Experience, I talked about the knowledge required to play on surfaces both indoor and outdoor. Outdoor surfaces include those from the very heavy greens in the northern hemisphere to the very fast surfaces of the southern hemisphere, and to a lesser extent synthetic surfaces.

What about your grip, stance and delivery?

Very early on in the course, in the section on Mechanics, we discussed the cradle and claw grips and finger grips. The claw grip is used mainly on heavier surfaces and by a person with a small hand who can't grip the bigger bowls so well. With the cradle grip you possibly don't get the same touch. The claw is

the grip mainly used throughout the world and the finger grip is the one used on fast surfaces.

If you use a cradle grip then you use it for all surfaces because you cannot hold the bowl in any other way unless you are a person who only plays on the very heavy surfaces. If you are one of those bowlers then possibly, if you found yourself on the very fast surfaces in Australia and New Zealand, then you would, in time, adapt your grip to suit.

You would also find it easier to adopt the new technique on the faster surfaces as the fear of the bowl slipping is offset by the minimal effort required to propel it the length of the green. Better touch would be developed by using either the claw or the finger grip.

But it isn't just a question of adjusting grip; you have to adjust stance to suit the pace of the green and your speed of delivery. In adjusting your stance you will automatically adjust backswing and the compensatory step, which relates directly to the delivery of any bowl – remembering that a bowler starts his backswing before he moves his foot. In other words the step follows the backswing and not vice-versa.

So when you step on to a green you have to change your game slightly according to conditions. If it's a heavy green you should know that you have to grip the bowl more firmly, take a longer backswing and use a far more upright stance.

If, however, you are playing bowls in Australia or New

On the fast greens of New Zealand you need to adopt a crouching stance with a slower delivery and a short step off the mat.

Note how the stance is slightly taller for medium-paced greens . . .

An example of bowls in South Africa – this is the Dube Club in Soweto. In the Republic, the greens are often medium-paced, faster than in Britain, but not as fast as in Australia and New Zealand.

Zealand then adjustments will be necessary to suit conditions. You would have to rest the bowl more in your hands, probably use the claw or finger grip, use a more crouching stance and not put anything like as much weight forward over the bowl when delivering. Therefore, your step will be much shorter and the speed of delivery will have to be in keeping with the pace of the green – a much slower and more deliberate action although still rhythmical.

This is the hardest part; to deliver at a different pace, particularly slower, and still keep the rhythm.

On the slower greens of the northern hemisphere the delivery action is so quick that it is difficult to see that the front foot is firmly placed on the g reen before the bowl is grounded. In fact, on very heavy greens it appears simultaneous. However, as the green speed increases, every second sees a more definite variation as the degree of forward bodyweight is reduced accordingly.

Bowlers who have played on the fast Australian greens and the ultra fast surfaces in New Zealand will be aware that there is a marked pause from when the front foot is planted to when the bowl makes contact with the green. This is employed to restrict forward bodyweight and coaches recommend that the right knee should be dropped as low as is necessary to allow only sufficient forward movement to achieve the correct follow through. The degree of pause and the distance that the right knee is lowered is obviously determined by the speed of the green or, to put it another way, the propulsion that is required to deliver the bowl from mat to jack.

Players used to heavy greens have great problems in reducing forward bodyweight and slowing down the speed of

. . . while on the slower greens of the northern hemisphere an upright stance is required with faster delivery and the front foot placed firmly forward.

Adapting to playing conditions

The author competing in the 1978 Commonwealth Games in Canada, where he won the singles gold medal.

A typical Maori greeting in New Zealand at the Okahu Bay club, near Auckland.

Bowling, Californian-style, where the greens are often set in dramatic and picturesque locations.

their action yet still maintain that vital factor – rhythm. Conversely, bowlers brought up on very fast surfaces are used to delivering with little effort and are not really aware that forward bodyweight is necessary on the heavier greens. Speeding up the action with a longer backswing and naturally a longer step will enable the player to reach the head but does not necessarily create rhythm. Rhythm in delivery is achieved through combining correctly the following factors – height of stance, length of backswing with compensatory step, forward bodyweight and speed of action.

Choice of bowls comes into it as well. The larger the bowl the better it behaves in the British Isles. I think this has always been accepted, although I would take it one stage further. The larger the bowl, the better it behaves on greens with more hazards. In other words it tends to be less affected by greens that haven't been rolled, with a lot of thatch in them, or are not cut down sufficiently.

The bigger the object, the better it's going to hold the line under these conditions. You can, of course, have extra weight by using a 'heavyweight' type bowl – but this is not quite the same. The bigger bowl also has a larger circumference so therefore, under given conditions, it will run on that much further than a smaller bowl. Each revolution on a heavier green will take the large bowl that much further than the smaller bowl.

If you compare a large bowl in the standard or medium weight with the same size bowl of the heavyweight type, say size six, you will find that in the northern hemisphere the standard or medium weight bowl delivered with the same control will travel further because it doesn't bite into the green quite like the heavier weight bowl.

So you will find on the heavier greens that the heavyweight bowl has its limitations and on greens that run at about 12 seconds or less I would not advocate using a heavyweight bowl, except in the smaller sizes.

If a person has a small hand and can only use a bowl of less than a five inch (size five), then I would possibly advocate the use of a heavyweight – and then it would depend on the conditions. If the green was running at 13 seconds plus, then it would be an advantage. It is an advantage for a bowler who has to use the smaller sizes to have the heavyweight bowl at his disposal because if you haven't got the weight then there is a possible disadvantage.

Nevertheless, it is much easier to get a size four standard weight up the green than a similar size heavyweight bowl if the speed is under 12 seconds. It depends on the surface. If you were playing in the southern hemisphere, on very fast surfaces, you would find that the size four heavyweight would go further than the size four medium weight.

Quite where the transition stage is I'm not sure, but I would think around 13 to 14 seconds. It really boils down to one thing – just how much the bowl bites into the green.

So the criteria on the choice of bowl is simply this. I would use a heavyweight bowl on slower greens of the northern hemisphere if I used sizes one to four. If I was playing in the southern hemisphere I would use the heavyweight bowl purely to offset windy conditions. I think if you use sizes six and seven you have enough weight anyway, although thoughts are evenly divided on this among bowlers from those countries in the southern hemisphere.

You will notice that I have not mentioned those who use size five bowl, which is perhaps one of the most popular sizes.

Competing here in Australia against Queenslander Keith Poole, on the fast green at Beaumaris near Melbourne.

Adapting to playing conditions

In Florida, the tropical climate does not suit the growing of grass for greens, so in many places the Americans bowl on a rubico surface – a fine slate substance (above) mixed with a binder and thinly spread over a porous surface to produce an excellent wide draw into the jack.

Below: Barrie Swannie from Croydon, Surrey, joined a tour from Bowls International magazine in 1982 and adapted to the rubico conditions magnificently to win the U.S. Open singles.

In this case the decision is borderline and will be a personal one with the player concerned, although I think that many of them would prefer the heavyweight bowl.

On very fast greens, wind is a factor that has to be considered. The small bowl with the extra density certainly performs better simply because there is less surface area to be affected and each revolution will not take the bowl as far. On these surfaces you tend to get more touch bowling.

The size that you select is governed by conditions.

Another factor is bias. I know that this word often covers a multitude of sins; all bowls are 'bias three' but some turn more than others. If you are going to play on fast surfaces where there is going to be big arc, then you will get more than an adequate arc if you use a narrower drawing bowl. It doesn't mean to say that because you have a narrower drawing bowl that you are going to take a narrow arc. It just means that you are going to take a big arc but not as big as some of the other bowlers.

If, however, you are playing on greens in the northern

Right: Action during the 1982 Commonwealth Games at Moorooka, Australia, where the greens were ultra fast.

hemisphere which are heavy and holding you will need a bowl that is taking a wider arc to draw round other bowls. On a grassy green in the northern hemisphere that is tracking – that is getting grooved – you don't want a bowl that is going on the outside edge of the track but one that sits nicely in the track.

If you are going to be playing on fresh grass each day – here I am thinking of tournaments which run over several days – then you might well decide to play with an average biased bowl which gives you plenty of arc. Again you have to consider the type of game you are playing. Is it a singles match or a team game?

If playing singles you may well go for a narrower bias bowl. In the case of a team game you may want that little bit of extra bias to draw round bowls or to play running shots.

Knowledge of the green will, of course, help to make these various selections. For instance, if I am playing bowls in New Zealand I certainly wouldn't take my own bowls with me. I would select a set which was more suitable to the conditions. When last there I used a size five standard weight bowl, whereas I normally use a size six (5 1/16"). My thinking behind this was quite simple. Using the size five I had got reasonable weight, just one size down on what I normally use. I took a chance on the wind and used them most successfully. I won all my section games but unfortunately, in a semi-final match with Nick Unkovitch, it started to blow, I lost my line a bit and lost a close match.

On reflection a heavyweight bowl might have been useful, but you don't always make the right decision.

You do gain experience playing on all these different surfaces and this applies to indoor as well. You will soon get to know whether or not you will need to bowl with a narrower or wider drawing bowl to get to your objective.

When I played in the Commonwealth Games, at Edmonton in Canada, I had heard that the greens were not of too good a standard – heavy with a lot of thatch. These greens usually show a lot of tracks after they have been played on. So I chose my bowls accordingly, choosing the narrowest drawing bowl I had, and it worked.

Self discipline

Contest of wills to emerge the victor

In the last chapter I spoke about how to tackle greens. How one tackles greens is in many ways related to how one tackles opponents. It is all part of your attitude to the game.

My own attitude has always been very positive and quite certainly never one of avoiding defeat, but always of beating the opponent. I am always thinking of the tactics whereby I can beat him. I concentrate on his mental weaknesses, trying to crack his game. The man with the stronger will to win nearly always emerges the winner.

However, you must not just think of yourself but gauge carefully each move and be confident that you can carry it out. You must approach each shot with certainty for it to be successfully achieved.

A player has to be constantly thinking about winning and he must refuse to be shaken by the 'rubs' of the green. It is fatal to let a little bit of bad luck disturb you. Somewhere along the line it will happen in your favour. Your attitude must be to say – 'I'll put these shots back on the next end, or with the next bowl'.

Never allow your opponent the slightest inkling that he is causing you any worry. When you recover the lost shots he may well believe that his own form and control is beginning to slip. Always appear confident and in control of the situation, even though the best laid schemes can sometimes go astray.

In any situation you will have to make an assessment of the percentages and if you always play to be on the right side, you will give yourself the best chance of winning – even when luck enters into it.

I must admit that my game is based on percentages of chance. I always weigh up what I am going to get out of a situation and what I am going to lose by it. If I consider the chances to be odds-on, that is, I stand to get more out of it than I stand to lose, I think it may be worth a chance.

So as well as training your mind to consider only the relevant factors concerning a shot, or any situation on a particular end, you must also play to some sort of plan – particularly when in trouble. If I have a good shots lead and we're nearing the end of the game, then I won't take any chances at all. I think the time to take chances is in the first 12 ends. My aim is to build a big lead early on. Then if I play a silly shot and give two or three away when I might have scored, I had calculated the risk and considered I had a chance to gain more than I would have given away. It would not have been a silly shot if I had achieved my aim!

I also try to unsettle my opponent psychologically. For instance, I sometimes let fly with a drive, especially if he has a cluster round the jack. I hope that my drive will discourage him from doing that too often and he, by playing positional bowls, will leave me room to draw to the jack. Even if my drive does not connect, I take great pains to ensure that I am very close. More often than not in these circumstances I do hit the target – after all, it is big enough. This is all part of trying to pressurise your opponent.

But whatever decision you make regarding a shot, you must

always be positive. Take time in deciding which to play and its execution, but when on the mat have the shot all worked out in your mind and settle on what strength should be given and the land you will be taking. Every shot has its perfect strength, but it may well be a toss-up whether or not it is advisable to play it at perfect strength or with a little extra weight. You have a strength that is easiest to play, which you find most comfortable and natural. It may be fast, medium or even just over a draw, but it is true for every bowler and this applies for coming on to another bowl.

Sometimes if you are playing a shot and impart just the right strength to, say, wrest out a bowl, you may also carry the jack to score shots. On the other hand it may be so vital to obtain shot that the question of scoring several is relatively unimportant.

It is all a question of priorities. For example, if I was winning by eight shots and there was a chance of ditching the jack for six, or an easy draw for a single, I might go for the six-count chance because if I succeed the match would be nearly over. But there is no hard and fast rule. If the other team was leading by four, holding shot and with the last bowl, it might be a different matter. The number of ends played would also come into the argument.

There is a definite difference in playing one type of shot at the start of the match, to playing the same shot in the latter ends. When the game draws to an end you can't take great chances.

One thing you must do when playing is shut out all distractions. It is all very well being relaxed, but avoid wandering off the rink and chatting to other people. Besides affecting your own playing, it may distract that of your partners.

Much is spoken about 'Lady Luck', but I think it is something you must ignore completely.

The game is a psychological battle. You will hear many bowlers talking about (and many cursing) the 'wicks' which went against them – they rarely talk about those that go for them. Misfortunes seem to stick in some people's minds more than anything else. This indicates a lack of confidence and poor

A cartoon parody of Bryant the Yoga disciple. As part of general preparation it can contribute to correct attitude and self-awareness.

Firing is one of Bryant's tactics for unsettling an opponent. An example was against Irishman Brenden McBrien (below) whose superb drawing power during an indoor international was repeatedly destroyed by the Bryant drive.

Self discipline

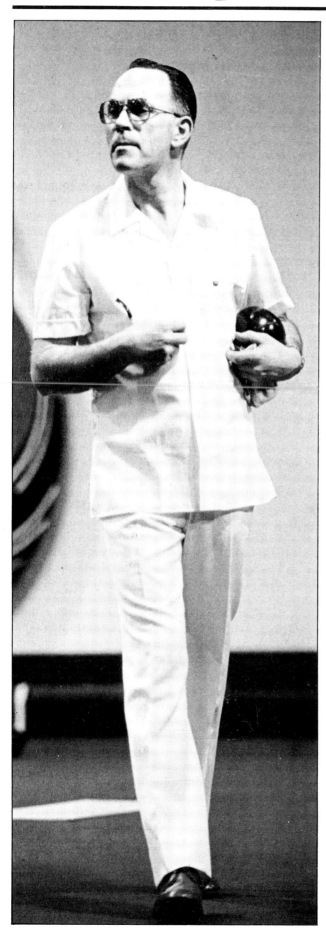

temperament. To dwell on things like that is the worst and most dangerous form of distraction.

There are many other distractions that can affect your play. Always remember that the game on your rink should be the only one in your mind, although I know that in such team games as the Middleton Cup, where the successes and failures of other rinks can affect the outcome, it is not always easy to keep your mind solely on your match.

It is worth remembering that while you may be technically perfect, tactically brilliant and physically fit, you need three other key factors – concentration, nerve and temperament.

I will be going over the mental approach and determination in the next chapters, so I won't touch on these aspects here. But it is well to remember two last points on self-discipline: Do not worry about your game too much and study each head carefully. They may seem like a slight contradiction in terms but you must make your own judgements. There will be many around the green free with advice, but you must assess the situation, look at all the percentages and play your shots with the utmost confidence – without worrying too much. The shots you play will be based on knowledge of the rink and that is the most important factor for it is you who is delivering the bowl.

The will to win is a state of mind and, added to natural skill, can help make a champion. You must sometimes forget surroundings and allow your mind to dwell purely on the business of the game. Every bowl has its value. Don't sacrifice the value of that bowl by being too hurried in your delivery. Take your time and visit the head if in doubt.

Lastly, you must remember that no matter how scrupulously you pay attention to all the details of technique, fitness, psychology and all other aspects, actual improvement comes with hours spent on the green.

Match-play develops judgement and experience, but knowledge gained from books, discussion, watching films or studying top class players in action can only be tested and filtered into your game by practice. Practice is not only essential to the beginner or novice keen to improve, but it is equally vital to the international or Middleton/Liberty county competition players keen to maintain form.

There is only one place to put right your faults, and that's on the green. So here is my guide to self-discipline:

(1) Always keep cool and have constructive thoughts under pressure.

(2) Always appear confident and in control of the situation.

(3) Train your mind to consider only the relevant facts.

(4) Always play to a plan when you are in trouble.

(5) Try to pressurise your opponent.

(6) Take your time and always be positive in whatever shot you decide to play.

(7) Shut out all distractions.

(8) Don't worry too much about your game.

(9) Study each head carefully.

Apply these guidelines rigidly while you play and you will implant self-discipline into your game.

Mr Cool himself. 'Never allow your opponent the slightest inkling that he is causing you any worry.'

Determination

Fighting spirit and the right attitude

One of the points that attracts many people to play bowls is that it seems a relatively easy game when you first start. It obviously becomes more difficult when you achieve certain standards and wish to keep bettering them. It is usually when you are no longer playing just for pure enjoyment that temperament can begin to effect your play.

How often have you heard it said that certain players have lost matches because they are too temperamental? All of us have some temperament – it's just that some people have an even and well-controlled temperament while others are more volatile. Few players are saints and there are many factors that can set our mood prior to playing in an important match. The good players are the ones who can conquer life's little trials and tribulations and put them aside while they are on the green.

Your temperament is often something decided for you when you are born. The highly stung nervous child often stays that way into adult life. The quick tempered and the slow and ponderous stay that way too. There are exceptions. We often hear of 'late developers' – well sometimes we can alter our personalities/temperaments as we get older. Some will say that you tend to 'mellow' like a good wine with age!

People have repeatedly been chosen for top positions in business life because they were alleged to have the correct temperament. And this often applies to bowlers. It is also a known fact that most leading sportsmen have a tendency to be highly strung, although the etiquette instilled into most bowlers tends to keep any displays of rank bad temper down to the minimum.

I believe that a good bowler must possess a fighting spirit which breeds determination to succeed, plus the ability to take the good with the bad.

One of the first steps to sorting out your temperament is having a clear understanding of yourself. When you fully understand, then you can apply any remedies.

Clearly if you are one of nature's little worriers, prone to be nervous or a little melancholic when a few shots down, then you need plenty of reassurance. And if you are of a phlegmatic nature you may need a little bit of 'driving on' to produce your best.

You may be of a volatile nature with an imagination that runs wild on occasions and, like the other two types I've just mentioned, will probably be the type who puts so much effort into concentration that this heightened state becomes inhibitory. Learning how and when to relax is as important as learning how to concentrate.

Given that you know your own temperament and have learned how to handle it, you will need to condition your mind to bring out your best in match play. In an earlier chapter I showed you how I use Yoga to help keep my body and muscles supple and fit. Yoga is also used by many people as a medium of relaxation and controlled thinking.

You needn't go to these lengths but you will find it helps to have a mind that is 'free' to concentrate on bowling. It's no good thinking about that important order you lost at work when you're on the mat about to play a shot that could result in your being six down or two up!

In most sports players take great pains with their practice, particularly before games. I think here of cricketers having nets before a game and practicing catching on a catchers cradle. Bowlers somehow don't seem to do this quite so much, usually just turning up for a game and placing their bowls on the green.

It is very important that a player should approach all games with the correct attitude. He must be determined to give of his best, be sharp and alert and have had a good look at the state of the green and surrounding conditions. This is especially true of outdoor games.

Many bowlers panic when they get a few shots behind. Only the bowler who can relax and combat tension will be able to pick himself up. Some players improve when they get the lead, while others tend to ease-up when getting a few shots in front.

Let's consider the minds of those who a) are in the lead and b) those who are behind. If a player(s) is trailing, even close to defeat, the knowledge that defeat is imminent can be the spur he needs to get back into his rhythm. Unless you are up against a poor fighter, this fellow is likely to be extremely dangerous over the last few ends.

The man who is leading, however, will be itching to get the game over – so some tension may creep into his play. It's like the nervous nineties in cricket. Keep pegging away, playing the right shots and doing exactly what you have set out to do, always remaining confident, cool and collected.

To summarise you must have the following qualitites:

(1) The ability to raise your game at crucial times.
(2) Never give up despite the odds being heavily stacked against you.
(3) Always try to enter every match in the correct frame of mind.
(4) Never let past defeats influence your play.

The grim look of determination as Bryant strides towards his second world singles title at Frankston in 1980. One of his golden rules is to never give up, no matter how heavily the odds are stacked against you.

A good team member

Commitment and enjoyment harmonised

A successful team is a unit with all players combining in perfect harmony and thoroughly enjoying the exercise. To achieve this all members must appreciate the psychology of the game and think positively at all times.

There are some very obvious differences between playing singles and the team games of pairs, triples and fours. In singles the player is bowling for 50 per cent of the time. This percentage decreases as the number of players increase so that in fours you share the mat with seven other people.

It is, nevertheless, still important to maintain your concentration in the non-bowling moments as well as in the time that you are on the mat. It is especially difficult for leads and No.2s because after they have bowled their duties have finished until the conclusion of that particular end. The No.3s still have a specific task to perform after they have bowled and will be the skip's right-hand man while the lead and No.2 are bowling.

In most cases a lead will spend something like a minute actually bowling during a six/seven minute end, but he still needs to be involved as part of a team. He can do this by adopting a positive attitude towards encouraging his teammates. In team play there is often far too much time standing around saying nothing. Far better to acknowledge your teammates' good bowls and make your presence felt. This will help to boost the teams confidence.

Anyone who has ever seen the former Scottish international skip Harry Reston will know that one man's enthusiasm and genuine pleasure in his fellows' success can boost overall morale sky-high. Spontaneous enthusiasm can be worthy of many shots in the closing stages of a match.

Unfortunately such interest is far from common in everyday club bowls, which is a pity. If clubs could only take their bowls a little more seriously in this respect they could still show all the aspects of true sportsmanship and obtain even more pleasure from the game. There is a tremendous amount to be gained by becoming completely absorbed in a match. More, in my opinion, than just standing around idly chatting until it's your turn to bowl again.

There is also nothing unsporting in keenness and enthusiasm, providing it is genuine and spontaneous. It must have these qualities, because sometimes over-keenness springs from a desire to cry down opponents as much as lifting team-mates. You are then getting into the area of gamesmanship.

Accepting, then, the necessity for everyone to maintain concentration and to encourage all other members of the

Team competitions, such as England's prestigious Middleton Cup for county sides, demand good temperament from all players. Time spent actually bowling decreases as the number increases, so maintaining concentration in the longer nonbowling periods becomes more difficult.

A good team member

The agony and ecstacy of international team play. A prostrate Wyn Richards and two England team mates are transfixed by an incoming bowl from skip David Ward at Ayr. Celebrations are just about to start but turn to anguish as the target is narrowly missed and suddenly it's the Welsh opponents who claim victory.

A good team member

team to bowl as well as they can, what are the specific duties of each player in a fours side?

The first duty of a lead lies in placing the mat. On the first end he must do this in accordance with the laws of the game which dictate that the front edge should be six feet from the front of the ditch. It can be in any position up the green from this point – providing, of course, that the jack is a minimum 25 yards from the front edge of the mat.

What I would then require from a lead is two bowls right in the head which can be used for promoting, resting or running through, delivered from a mat position I would have chosen if I was lead. Here the lead must accept his skip's desire for a certain mat length and have consideration for his team as a unit and not what length he is best at.

In many ways the No. 2 is complementary to the lead and as such his task may be to achieve what the lead has failed to do, or simply to balance or improve a promising position.

The No. 2 is often not highly rated, but is a very important part of any fours team. He must be every bit as strong as the remainder of the team and often possess extra qualities of patience. This is required because a No. 2 often has to bowl to 'blank' positions rather than a clearly visible target.

If the shot is against him the No.2 is normally asked to play a specific shot; if not he must put two useful bowls into the head making sure that he has sized-up the swing of the green.

I would always choose a No. 3 who can play a fast bowl and

Consultation, concentration and celebration – three imperatives for the good team member. Scotland's David Gourlay, John Watson and Dennis Love study a head; regular partner to David Bryant, commentator David Rhys-Jones, puts everything into his shot; and happy Scots acclaim success on the run

one who is adept at all of the game's shots. Obviously I would hope to find a good all-rounder, but at club level it is often difficult to find the complete player. If the lead and No. 2 are reasonable length bowlers then they should be able to get something close to the jack and it is always an easier task for a No. 3 to have some kind of target or resting place at which to aim.

A No.3 will offer advice to his skip, but only when necessary. If the position has altered after the skip left the head or the No. 3 feels that another inspection of the head is called for, then fine. But nothing can be more infuriating for a skip than to be on the mat preparing to bowl and then be suddenly interrupted by the No. 3 dancing around and shouting fresh advice.

The skip of the rink must watch every move on the board, assessing the strengths and weaknesses of the opposition, and drag out every ounce of skill from his other team. The skip must discover the best way of motivating each member. One may need encouragement, one flattery, while another might be a little impetuous and need to be curbed.

Skips are in complete charge of a rink and, while listening to the thoughts of colleagues, must have a definite shot in mind when stepping on the mat. To still be in two minds at this stage can be fatal.

On the playing side, I think it goes without saying that the skip must be capable of playing all shots and have a great deal

A good team member

of experience. It is not sufficient just to be a consistent bowler; a skip must have the knowledge of building a head and managing a rink.

There will always be the two types of skip – the adventurous and the cautious. Choose the style best suited to your skills and give it a good trial. Always bear in mind that bowls should be a pleasurable game. Over-caution can spoil that pleasure as your game could become negative.

We have dealt with the individuals in the rink, so what are the points to remember for making a good team member?

(1) Be a player everyone enjoys having on the rink.

(2) Only praise – never criticise. When a player is on the mat about to deliver his bowl he should feel that he has the backing of every member of the team. This applies particularly to the skip who always has to play more pressure bowls than any other member of the team.

(3) A good skip discusses tactics with his team. However, he has to make the final decisions and cannot please everybody, so whatever he decides he must know he has the confidence of his fellow team members.

(4) Be a confidence booster. If you are a skip, never forget that however off-form a member of the rink may be, no player ever deliberately steps on to the mat to deliver a bad bowl. Always try to help by discussing the playing conditions, by introducing a little humour to relieve the tension, by thinking deeply about the player's problems and therefore, hopefully, devising a tactical solution.

(5) Do not be a selfish player. Always consider what is best for the team. What you like personally may not be best for the unit. This applies particularly to the lead with the placing of mat and jack.

(6) Listen to all instructions carefully and be quite clear what is required of you. Endeavour to comply with your skip's requests, giving full concentration and effort when delivering the bowl even if the shot is not your personal choice.

(7) A good skip is amenable, approachable, has a sense of humour, always appears relaxed, encourages and helps his players. No member of a four should ever have to think twice about discussing tactics with his skip, but if his suggestion is not accepted he must realise that it was only discarded after careful consideration. He must then accept the decision and not let it affect his game.

(8) Harmony is the key to success and this can be achieved by open discussion off the rink. As a skip I like all my players to be aware of basic standards which are required and have already been listed.

(9) Be conversant with the laws of the game.

Following pages: Sporting applause from both sides for a shot well played.

Right and below: Let's dance! The harmony of a team finds ultimate expression in the pleasure of winning. But it must also hold fast in defeat.

Sportsmanship

Sportsmanship

The present generation of bowlers have every reason to thank those pioneers who not only formulated the present rules, but were largely responsible for introduction of the many 'unwritten laws' which are still today regarded as the etiquette of the game.

Friendships made on the bowling green are sincere and enduring. This is what gives our game its special charm. Proceedings are commence with a friendly handshake and introductions all round with first name terms being observed – a familiarity which creates an atmosphere of warmth and friendship.

The code ensures that a new club member will feel at home at once. It also ensures that no circumstances will give one bowler an unfair advantage over another. On the green all players are regarded as equal.

A pleasing gesture at the start of any game will be to hand the jack to your opponent if he takes the mat first. It is also a sporting gesture to commend a good bowl of your opponent's and of a player in your own team. You should find that this immediate token will be reciprocated.

It is also etiquette to acknowledge a fluke or good rub, bearing in mind that all players have them at some time or other during their bowling lives.

Sometimes players, quite subconsciously, follow their bowls up the green in such a manner as to obliterate the view of the running from their opponent. Although not a breach of rules in most countries, it is quite easy to step to one side to allow an opponent sight of your bowls path up the green.

Players should also remember when their bowl has stoped running – time being allowed for the marking of 'touchers' – they should then give possession of the rink to their opponents and retire to a position behind the mat or behind the head.

You should never stand in any position that is likely to distract your opponent, nor do anything that will put him off when about to bowl.

A player should always keep to his own rink and not wander off to chat to other players or people on the bank. It could be distracting to other bowlers. Always pay attention to the end being played. Nothing will be more frustrating to other members of the team than to feel that you are not giving of your best because you are not concentrating fully.

Avoid wasting time arguing which is 'shot'. If there is any doubt the person asking for the shot should get down and measure. If in doubt – measure out, being a guiding principle. If you still cannot agree and an umpire is called for – keep well back. Let him get on with the job in hand and don't try to tell him how it should be done. Always remember that his decision is final.

When a skip decides to play a 'firing' shot it is not only common sense, but a good idea, to move well out of the line of fire, even to standing on the bank. This way players avoid being struck by any bowls or the jack that move quickly out of the head! Many unpleasant situations have arisen by players not observing these very basic rules.

In the last chapter, I dealt with the attitudes of each player in the rink towards being a good team member. Each player must observe these points as well as the etiquette of the game.

The skip of a rink bears special responsibility. A skip should never hold any player open to ridicule by shouting what is often blatantly obvious. 'You're short – you're narrow' said in a sarcastic manner can only cause friction. Informing a player

that 'he needs to put a yard more on his next bowl' in a quiet, efficient manner is constructive and reassuring.

Players know when they have bowled a 'bad un' – they don't need reminding.

Constant encouragement is the keynote of success, always giving full recognition for the good shots. One of the worst crimes that any skip can commit is to miss a good shot played by one of his team because he was chatting to his opposing skip or spectators.

The worst crime of all is for a skip to turn his back on a team-member who has just delivered a bad bowl.

Skips should also avoid showing an experienced player what green to take. With novices it is obviously necessary, but the more experienced players will consider it something of an insult if a skip stands in a position and says 'use my feet as your line'.

The skip is in control of the rink at all times but if he cannot control without being a despot he should not skip.

Any skip worth his position in the team realises that there is good sense at both ends of the rink and uses his team to full advantage. If a player can't quite see the shot he is being asked to play, the skip should keep advising him of its necessity, even asking him to come up to the head and inspect.

While this will help, there should never be any doubt as to who is in control of the game. The skip is responsible for every shot played and should never try to duck that responsibility.

Always try to be on time for a game, and if unexpectedly delayed try and get a message to your opponent. It will be appreciated.

The ability to win and lose gracefully is also a very important part of good etiquette. We have all heard certain players referred to as poor losers and a victory against a bowler who falls into this category is far from enjoyable as one usually has to hear all the excuses over a drink in the club house or the opponent remembers another urgent appointment and leaves immediately after the match. Fortunately the majority of bad

Narrowly defeated at the 1982 Embassy World Indoor Bowls Championship, Australian Jack Hosking concedes gracefully to David Bryant.

Sportsmanship

losers do, at least, have the courtesy to join the winners in a drink but they cannot bring themselves to accept the fact that on that day they were second best.

On the other hand the good sportsman has a positive philosophy in that he realises he cannot win all his games and lost games are water under the bridge. Such a player is a pleasure to play against and is doubly difficult to beat as his temperament is superb. But once beaten he goes out of his way to congratulate the victor and praise the manner in which the victory was achieved. He acknowledges that it is the other man's day and puts himself out to make it a memorable one although he may be bitterly disappointed with his own performance on that occasion.

Equally important, however, is how the victor conducts himself. If his philosophy is as sound as that of his opponent he will accept his win in a gracious manner, explaining that he had the rubs of the green at the crucial times etc. and go out of his way to tell his opponent that he played well but was unlucky.

In short, the golden rule of good sportsmanship is to be humble in victory and generous in defeat. Having said that there is a breed far worse than the bad losers. I refer, of course, to bad winners! These players are naturally egotistical and usually are equally unpopular on and off the green. There is nothing worse in any sport than to lose to a player who does not know how to conduct himself in victory.

The man who sings his own praises and tells his opponent that he was outclassed is very difficult to tolerate, even to the best of sportsmen, and to lose to this type of player is a real test of character. Thankfully such bowlers are few and far between as invariably they possess poor temperament themselves and are also the worst losers.

Any competitive bowler should always adopt the attitude that he should conduct himself in a similar manner to that which he would expect from his opponent. He should take pride in being respected for his sportsmanship and good

The good sportsman should also be a good ambassador and this young bowler will remember the day he received an award from the world champion.

etiquette and should never forget that having 'a good time' is more important than anything else.

Just as there is an etiquette in playing the game there is an etiquette in marking a match and to do either correctly it is important to be conversant with the laws of the game and the duties of a marker. A player, asked to mark a tie, should always remember he is there at the player's request, to supply information, mark touchers, remove dead bowls, keep the score, centre the jack etc. but he is not an umpire and has no authority to award shots. He may measure at the request of the players but it is for them to agree the score on that end. The only laws that he is required to enforce under the laws of the game are that the jack distance from the mat is of a correct length and that the bowls bear the official stamp.

Good markers are like good football referees in that they are inconspicuous until they are needed and they keep the game flowing. The following are a few points for markers which can be included in etiquette:

(1) A marker shall stand at one side of the rink and to the rear of the jack. He must remain still when a player is on the mat and be careful not to obscure rink boundary pegs.

(2) He should only volunteer information when asked and then in the manner as laid down in the laws of the game under duties of a marker.

(3) Unless requested his visits to the head should be as few as possible and only when necessary. The bowler must always be confident that the marker will not move during delivery.

(4) Between ends a good marker moves as quickly as he is able to keep the game flowing. Changing the scoreboard, rewinding a measure, etc are duties which can be done after the first delivery.

(5) He must never forget all decisions have to be agreed by both players e.g. dead bowls removed from ditch.

(6) Spectators moving on the bank are a distraction to the players and any help he can give to minimise this is appreciated.

(7) He must remain strictly neutral at all times.

To sum up the points on etiquette:

(1) Always dress correctly for all games.

(2) Compliment your opponent on a good bowl.

(3) Stand still when a player is about to bowl.

(4) Do not talk or make a noise behind the mat when a player is delivering.

(5) Remain behind the mat or behind the head when it is not your turn to play. As soon as your bowl comes to rest possession of the rink passes to your opponent.

(6) Keep to your own rink. Do not become a wanderer and distract other bowlers.

(7) On a bright sunny day be aware of your shadow. Do not let it mask the jack, nor permit it to fall in front of the mat when your opponent is about to deliver.

(8) Try to avoid obscuring boundary pegs, rink plates and markers.

(9) Never criticise – only praise.

(10) Pay attention to the game. Nothing can be more frustrating to your partners than to feel that you are not giving of your best through lack of concentration.

(11) Always appear that you are enjoying the game whatever the fortunes.

(12) Stand well back from the head when firing shots are played. If a jack or bowl makes contact with a player make sure that it's not you!

CHAPTER 22

Roots and nations

The game of bowls was probably derived from a popular game of the Ancient Egyptians which was played with skittles and rounded stones. Implements for playing a game were found in the tomb of an Egyptian child buried around 7,000 years ago and other examples have been found on sculptured vases, plaques and wall coverings of that period.

The game was popular with the Kings and Nobles of that era and was later adopted by other earlier civilizations in China, Greece and Rome. Indeed, when the Caesars' ruled over the Holy Roman Empire they played a game from which the Italians' present sport of Bocce has been derived.

Bowling games have been given a variety of names throughout the world – Bolla (Saxon), Bulla (Latin), Bolle (Danish), Boules (French), and the beautifully named Ula Miaka of Polynesian origin. These games were perhaps more connected with our present conception of skittles – but nevertheless certainly spawned our game of lawn bowls.

Although it is interesting to note that lawn bowls is hardly played in Europe at all now, yet it was from that continent that all the worldwide bowling games have spread. Introduced into Southern France from Greece and Rome, the bowls of antiquity has expanded and scattered throughout the world into four main forms.

The French games, grouped under Les Boules, which also includes Italian Bocce and some games played in South America, the skittles type games played in Austria and Germany, lawn bowling which reached England via the Baltic countries and lastly, curling which is played on ice-rinks in the UK, America, Canada and the Scandinavian countries.

Outside Europe, America is the oldest bowling continent. Bowls has been popular in America since colonial times. It was probably introduced by English settlers when early colonies like Virginia, Massachusetts, New Hampshire and the Carolinas were founded.

It is believed that the game was played in Massachusetts and Connecticut as far back as 1615. Certainly bowling was played at the Sturdevant Spalding Inn, New Hampshire, in 1632, and George Washington, America's first president, played bowls on his estate at Mount Vernon, Virginia.

Bowling in the United States in modern times has been mainly an activity enjoyed by retired people. It has yet to attract younger players to the same degree as other countries. Most of the bowling takes place during the day when young people are working and there are no indoor facilities.

Above: One of the author's old rivals from Hong Kong, Philip Chok.

Left: One of the most popular outposts for bowls is Western Samoa, whose Asenati Vaeau is seen here competing in the 1982 Brisbane Games.

Roots and nations

Florida is a popular venue for winter visitors from Canada and the northern states and bowling often takes place on a synthetic shale-type surface called rubico and sometimes under floodlights. The few grass greens tend to be slow and erratic. In view of its small number of participants America's record in the 1972 World Championships, held in Worthing, was remarkable.

Jim Candelet finished fifth in the singles and partnered by Bill Tewkesbury was silver medallist in the pairs, and Bill Miller, Tewkesbury was silver medallist in the pairs, and Bill Miller Clive Forester and Dick Folkins won the triples gold. Fifth place in the pairs saw them finish in third spot for the Leonard team trophy, won that year by Scotland.

Apart from a primitive type of bowling played by Indians in British Columbia, bowling began in Canada in 1734 at Nova Scotia.

In 1734 an enclosure was reserved as a green for the officer

Left: One of the United States' leading players among their 6,000 bowlers is Neil McInnes.
Below: Silver medallist in both the 1978 Commonwealth Games and 1980 World championships was John Snell, one of Australia's all time greats.

of the garrison of Annapolis (Royal), while the Duke of Kent, grandfather of Edward VII, also had a green laid in his grounds at Prince's Lodge, Bedford Basin, Halifax, around the same time.

In 1870 Ontario became the main centre for the game and in 1896 the Western Ontario Bowling Association was founded. Bowling in Canada is now under the control of the Canadian Lawn Bowling Council, which was established in 1924 and is a full member of the International Bowling Board.

The nine provinces in Canada are affiliated to the council, although the numbers of bowlers in each province varies considerably. One has only 103 members while Ontario has 6,000!

Many of Canada's younger players are making a mark on the world scene and with government aid the sport is beginning to flourish, with a start being made on the indoor scene. Canada also has a great number of women bowlers and staged the Women's World Championships at Willowdale, Ontario, in 1981.

Flat green bowls is one of Australia's major sports with over half-a-million participants. No doubt the popularity of the game is based on the Australian's love of outdoor activities but another major factor in its development has been the favourable climate, which enables bowls to be played outdoor throughout the year in Queensland, New South Wales and Northern Territory.

Bowls was introduced into Australia in 1844 when a green was opened at the Beach Tavern, Sandy Bay, Tasmania. This was soon followed by greens at Sydney, in Victoria and at certain hotels in the suburbs of Melbourne.

These provided the basis for the development of the game and the oldest club still in existence is Melbourne B.C. which was founded in 1864.

Australia is proud of the fact that the Imperial Bowling Association, the forerunner of the English Bowling Association, was formed in 1899 at the instigation of Australian bowlers, who accompanied the Australian cricket team that year.

The Australian Bowling Council, which controls the game in Australia today, was founded at Melbourne in 1911 with a total membership of 8,352. It is responsible for the administration of the men's game, the women having their own body which operates in a similar manner. The ABC, within the regulations of the International Bowling Board, has its own set of laws which vary slightly in some cases. But generally they have their origin in those of the Scottish Bowling Association.

The Australian national championships attract a mammoth entry and play is spread over two weeks, with the interstate series taking up four days of the previous week. It is not unusual for over 2,500 players to enter the singles, 1,300 for the pairs and over 1,000 for the fours.

Mostly the Australian greens consist of seven rinks and there are no 'strings' as there are in the UK. The minimum jack length is 66ft, not 75ft as in the UK.

Since the Commonwealth Games in London in 1934, Australia has been represented everytime that bowls has been played and staged the first World Bowls series in 1966 near Sydney. They won the first ever international event during this championship with successes in the pairs (gold) and triples (gold) taking the team trophy as well. The Australians have continued to make their marks on the world scene since and took the Commonwealth Games fours gold at the 1982 games.

Canada has little or no indoor bowling facilities to use during their winter, so it's quite an achievement when players like Barrie McFadden perform so well in international events.

Former Rugby player Peter Belliss has made a big impact on the world game with his ferocious firing technique and is one of New Zealand's leading professionals.

Roots and nations

The Ancient Polynesians, including those that migrated to New Zealand some 600 years ago, certainly had bowling games. But the modern game was probably introduced in the country 120 years ago by a group of Scottish settlers who made their home at Auckland, North Island.

It was, however, in Dunedin on South Island that the game really secured a foothold. A well-known Wellington merchant, imported a set of bowls for himself and on hearing that a gold strike had been made at Gabriel's Gully on South Island, decided to pack his bags and move to the Otago area. He opened a business at Dunedin in 1862 and demonstrated his skill at bowls to his customers. In 1871 such interest was shown in the game that the Dunedin Bowls and Quoits Club was formed.

In 1886 the stage was set for the formation of the New Zealand Bowling Association with eight clubs from the South Island and two from the north. The association's first championships were held in its inaugural year, attracting 28 rinks. Development of the game has become quite rapid with a total membership of over 55,000 from 636 clubs split over the two islands which rises by approximately 1,000 members a year.

New Zealand has competed in all the bowls events of the Empire later Commonwealth Games, winning six gold, seven silver and three bronze medals.

The New Zealand greens are unique in the world, the majority having the cotula weed surface. The advantages of the cotula surface are that it wears better, is not affected by weather and there is no expense on seed. It is, however, a lot faster than normal grass surfaces but even after heavy rain is

Left: South African Doug Watson won the world singles in 1976, but was unable to defend it in either Frankston (1980) or Aberdeen (1984).

Right: Israel's best known bowler is Cecil Bransky, a former South African singles, and Australian fours champion before emigrating to the Middle East.

Below: One of the surprises of the 1982 Brisbane Games, was the fourth place in the singles achieved by Garin Beare the champion of Zimbabwe where they have just 75 clubs.

consistent in pace.

The area under the jurisdiction of the South African Bowling Association is vast – 25 times that of England – and its first bowling club was opened in 1884. South Africa can rightly claim to be the first country to introduce women to bowling. The Kimberley Club, opened in 1892, gave women permission to practice on the green.

The lack of railways probably hindered development at the turn of the century but in 1904 the inaugural meeting of the South African Bowling Association was held with 11 clubs joining. Development was then hastened by the encouragement given by the Chamber of Mines which recommended bowls as a healthy recreation. Apart from mining districts, greens were laid out in public parks.

Growth was fairly rapid after the First World War with 79

clubs and 5,000 members in 1922 to 210 clubs and 9,500 in 1936. The biggest expansion period was the 10 years from 1944-54 when the number of clubs and members nearly doubled.

South Africa has until recent years taken part in the Commonwealth Games, winning gold medals three times in the singles and twice in the fours.

The spread of bowls in South Africa was also to be felt in Rhodesia (now Zimbabwe), Swaziland, Zambia and Malawi and into north Africa in Kenya. All these countries are members of the International Bowling Board and compete in both Commonwealth and World Championships.

It can therefore be seen that the game of bowls knows no international boundaries and year by year the list of countries playing the flat green game is growing.

Today some 26 countries are regular participants, among them the Pacific islands of Papua New Guinea, Fiji and Western Samoa. Hong Kong also has a small but powerful number of both male and female members who achieved some remarkable wins in recent world events, capturing the Commonwealth Games fours and pairs gold in Edmonton 1978.

In recent years Japan and Israel have stepped on to the world bowls scene and in the mid-1950's a green was laid at the Genval English Country Club in Belgium. Spain also has one grass green – the First Lawn Bowls Club at Fuengirola – and others are planned at such places as Almeria.

The South American Bowling Federation was formed in 1944 to look after the development of the game in that continent although bowls has in fact been played in Argentina since the early 1900s in the Buenos Aires region. The Lima Cricket and Football Club of Peru includes a bowls green among its facilities. And two of the Channel Islands, Jersey and Guernsey, are included in the 25 members of the IBB.

Left: Fijian determination expressed by Maria Lum On during the 1982 Brisbane Games. Above: Hong Kong's 1983 Kodak Masters champion George Souza, with Linda King, the crown colony's World Championship triples gold medallist in 1981.

Laws of the game

TO ENJOY the game of bowls fully all bowlers should be fully conversant with the laws of the game. After all, it is these laws that form the framework for the game that you play.

It was not until 1849, that a complete Code of Laws was drawn up by clubs in the West of Scotland under the direction of **W W Mitchell** a Glasgow solicitor and keen bowler.

Mitchell's laws were adopted by all clubs in the West of Scotland and later by the Scottish Bowling Association when it was formed in 1893. Later still, in 1905, the International Bowling Board was formed and adopted the Scottish B.A. laws.

The laws of the flat green game in all parts of the world are substantially founded on the laws that Mitchell drafted and issued in 1849.

It is these laws that are printed here for which I acknowledge the kind permission of the IBB for their reproduction.

There are variations of course to these laws and the English Bowling Federation code, which is played in 10 counties covering East Anglia, East Midlands and the North have five basic differences from the IBB laws.

1. There are no 'Touchers'.
2. Only bowls within six feet of the jack can be counted for shots.
3. Players may alter the order in which they play after each completed end.
4. In rink play, three players constitute a rink.
5. The front edge of the mat may be moved up to 12 feet from the front edge of the ditch.

DEFINITIONS

1. (a) "Controlling Body" means the body having immediate control of the conditions under which a match is played. The order shall be:
   (i) The International Bowling Board,
   (ii) The National Bowling Association,
   (iii) The State, Division, Local District or County Association,
   (iv) The Club on whose Green the Match is played.

   (b) "Skip" means the Player, who, for the time being, is in charge of the head on behalf of the team.

   (c) "Team" means either a four, triples or a pair.

   (d) "Side" means any agreed number of Teams, whose combined scores determine the results of the match.

   (e) "Four" means a team of four players whose positions in order of playing are named, Lead, Second, Third, Skip.

   (f) "Bowl in Course" means a bowl from the time of its delivery until it comes to rest.

   (g) "End" means the playing of the Jack and all the bowls of all the opponents in the same direction on a rink.

   (h) "Head" means the Jack and such bowls as have come to rest within the boundary of the rink and are not dead.

   (i) "Mat Line" means the edge of the Mat which is nearest to the front ditch. From the centre of the Mat Line all necessary measurements to Jack or bowls shall be taken.

   (j) "Master Bowl" means a bowl which has been approved by the I.B.B. as having the minimum bias required, as well as in all other respects complying with the Laws of the Game and is engraved with the words "Master Bowl".
      (i) A Standard Bowl of the same bias as the Master Bowl shall be kept in the custody of each National Association.
      (ii) A Standard Bowl shall be provided for the use of each official Licensed Tester.

   (k) "Jack High" means that the nearest portion of the Bowl referred to is in line with and at the same distance from the Mat Line as the nearest portion of the Jack.

   (l) "Pace of Green" means the number of seconds taken by a bowl from the time of its delivery to the moment it comes to rest, approximately 30 yards from the Mat Line.

   (m) "Displaced" as applied to a Jack or Bowl means "disturbed" by any agency that is not sanctioned by these laws.

   (n) A 'set of bowls' means four bowls all of which are the same manufacture, and are of the same size, weight, colour and serial number where applicable.

THE GREEN

2. **The Green – Area and Surface:**
   The Green should form a square of not less than 40 yards and not more than 44 yards a side. It shall have a suitable playing surface which shall be level. It shall be provided with suitable boundaries in the form of a ditch and bank.

3. **The Ditch**
   The Green shall be surrounded by a ditch which shall have a holding surface not injurious to bowls and be free from obstacles. The ditch shall be not less than 8 inches not more than 15 inches wide and it shall be not less than 2 inches not more than 8 inches below the level of the green.

4. Banks

The bank shall be not less than 9 inches above the level of the green, preferably upright, or alternatively at an angle of not more than 35 degrees from the perpendicular. The surface of the face of the bank shall be non-injurious to bowls. No steps likely to interfere with play shall be cut in the banks.

5. Division of the Green

The Green shall be divided into spaces called rinks, each not more than 19 feet, not less than 18 feet wide. They shall be numbered consecutively, the centre line of each rink being marked on the bank at each end by a wooden peg or other suitable device. The four corners of the rinks shall be marked by pegs made of wood, or other suitable material, painted white and fixed to the face of the bank and flush therewith or alternatively fixed on the Bank not more than four inches back from the face thereof. The corner pegs shall be connected by a green thread drawn tightly along the surface of the green, with sufficient loose thread to reach the corresponding pegs on the face or surface of the bank, in order to define the boundary of the rink.

White pegs or discs shall be fixed on the side banks to indicate a clear distance of 76 feet from the ditch on the line of play. Under no circumstances shall the boundary thread be lifted while the bowl is in motion. The boundary pegs of an outside rink shall be placed at least two feet from the side ditch. *(EBA ruling only: For 76 feet read 27 yards).*

6. Permissible Variations of Laws 2 and 5

(a) National Associations may admit Greens in the form of a square not longer than 44 yards, nor shorter than 33 yards, or of a rectangle of which the longer side should not be more than 44 yards and the shorter side not less than 33 yards.

(b) For domestic play the Green may be divided into Rinks, not less than 14 feet not more than 19 feet wide. National Associations may dispense with the use of boundary threads.

MAT, JACK, BOWLS, FOOTWEAR

7. Mat

The Mat shall be of a definite size, namely 24 inches long and 14 inches wide.

8. Jack

The Jack shall be round and white, with a diameter of not less than 2-15/32nd inches, nor more than 2-17/32nd inches, and not less than 8 ounces, nor more than 10 ounces in weight.

9. Bowls

(a)

(i) Bowls shall be made of wood, rubber or composition and shall be black or brown in colour and each bowl of the set shall bear the member's individual and distinguishing mark on each side. The provision relating to the distinguishing mark on each side of the bowl need not apply other than in International Matches, World Bowls Championships and Commonwealth Games.

Bowls made of wood (lignum vitae) shall have a maximum diameter of 5¼ins (133.35mm) and a minimum diameter of 4⅝ins (117mm) and the weight shall not exceed 3lb 8oz (1.59Kg). Loading of bowls made of wood is strictly prohibited.

(ii) For all International and Commonwealth Games Matches a bowl made of rubber or composition shall have a maximum diameter of 5⅛ inches and a minimum diameter of 4⅝ins (117mm) and the weight shall not exceed 3lb 8ozs.

Subject to bowls bearing a current stamp of the Board and/or a current stamp of a Member National Authority and/or the current stamp of the B.I.B.C. and provided they comply with the Board's Laws, they may be used in all matches controlled by the Board or by any Member National Authority.

Not withstanding the aforegoing provisions, any Member National Authority may adopt a different scale of weights and sizes of bowls to be used in matches under its own control – such bowls may not be validly used in International Matches, World Championships, Commonwealth Games or other matches controlled by the Board if they differ from the Board's Laws, and unless stamped with a current stamp of the Board or any Member National Authority or the B.I.B.C.

(iii) The controlling body may, at its discretion, supply and require players to temporarily affix an adhesive marking to their bowls in any competition game. Any temporary marking under this Law shall be regarded as part of the bowl for all purposes under these Laws.

b) **Bias of Bowls**

The Master Bowl shall have a Bias approved by the International Bowling Board. A Bowl shall have a Bias not less than that of the Master Bowl, and shall bear the imprint of the Stamp of the International Bowling Board, or that of its National Association. National Associations may adopt a standard which exceeds the bias of the Master bowl. To ensure accuracy of bias and visibility of stamp, all bowls shall be re-tested and re-stamped at least once every ten years, or earlier if the date of the stamp is not clearly legible. (B.I.B.C. ruling for domestic play only. For ten years read fifteen years for all bowls stamped or restamped from 1.1.1977). *(EBA ruling only: As from January 1, 1986 the re-stamping of bowls for competitive and domestic play in England is dispensed with. Bowls must, however, bear a legible stamp for 1985 or later, and can continue to be used without stamping until such time as the stamp becomes illegible.)*

c) **Objection to Bowls**

A challenge may be lodged by an opposing player and/or the official Umpire, and/or the controlling body.

A challenge or any intimation thereof shall not be lodged with any opposing player during the progress of a Match.

A challenge may be lodged with the Umpire at any time during a Match, provided the Umpire is not a Player in that or any other match of the same competition.

If a challenge be lodged it shall be made not later than ten minutes after the completion of the final

Laws of the game

end in which the Bowl was used.

Once a challenge is lodged with the Umpire, it cannot be withdrawn.

The challenge shall be based on the grounds that the bowl does not comply with one or more of the requirements set out in Law 9(a) and 9(b).

The Umpire shall request the user of the bowl to surrender it to him for forwarding to the Controlling body. If the owner of the challenged bowl refuses to surrender it to the Umpire, the Match shall thereupon be forfeited to the opponent. The user or owner, or both, may be disqualified from playing in any match controlled or permitted by the controlling body, so long as the bowl remains untested by a licensed tester.

On receipt of the bowl, the Umpire shall take immediate steps to hand it to the Secretary of the controlling body, who shall arrange for a table test to be made as soon as practicable, and in the presence of a representative of the controlling body.

If a table test be not readily available, and any delay would unduly interfere with the progress of the competition, then, should an approved green testing device be available, it may be used to make an immediate test on the Green. If a green test be made it shall be done by, or in the presence of the Umpire, over a distance of not less than 70 feet. The comparison shall be between the challenged bowl and a standard bowl, or if it be not readily available then a recently stamped bowl, of similar size or nearly so, should be used.

The decision of the Umpire, as a result of the test, shall be final and binding for that match.

The result of the subsequent table test shall not invalidate the decision given by the Umpire on the green test.

If a challenged bowl, after an official table test, be found to comply with all the requirements of Law 9(a) and (b), it shall be returned to the user or owner.

If the challenged bowl be found not to comply with Law 9(a) and (b), the match in which it was played shall be forfeited to the opponent.

If a bowl in the hands of a licensed tester has been declared as not complying with Law 9(a) and (b), by an official representative of the Controlling Body, then, with the consent of the owner, and at his expense, it shall be altered so as to comply before being returned to him.

If the owner refuses his consent, and demands the return of his bowl, any current official stamp appearing thereon shall be cancelled prior to its return.

(d) **Alteration to Bias**

A player shall not alter, or cause to be altered, other than by an official bowl tester, the bias of any bowl, bearing the imprint of the official stamp of the Board, under penalty of suspension from playing for a period to be determined by the Council of the National Association, of which his club is a member. Such suspension shall be subject to confirmation by the Board, or a committee thereof appointed for that

purpose, and shall be operative among all associations in membership with the Board.

10. **Footwear**

Players, Umpires and Markers shall wear white, brown or black smooth-soled heel-less footwear while playing on the green or acting as Umpires or Markers.

(E.B.A. ruling only: Brown footwear only will be worn).

ARRANGING A GAME

11. **General form and duration**

A game of bowls shall be played on one rink or on several rinks. It shall consist of a specified number of shots or ends, or shall be played for any period of time as previously arranged.

The ends of the game shall be played alternately in opposite directions excepting as provided in Laws 38, 42, 44, 46 and 47.

12. **Selecting the rinks for play**

When a match is to be played, the draw for the rinks to be played on shall be made by the skips or their representatives.

In a match for a trophy or where competing skips have previously been drawn, the draw to decide the numbers of the rinks to be played on shall be made by the visiting skips or their representatives.

No player in a competition or match shall play on the same rink on the day of such competition or match before play commences under penalty of disqualification.

This law shall not apply in the case of open Tournaments.

13. **Play arrangements**

Games shall be organised in the following play arrangements:

(a) As a single game.
(b) As a team game.
(c) As a sides game.
(d) As a series of single games, team games, or side games.
(e) As a special tournament of games.

14. A single game shall be played on one rink of a Green as a single handed game by two contending players, each playing two, three or four bowls singly and alternately.

15. A pairs game by two contending teams of two players called lead and skip according to the order in which they play, and who at each end shall play four bowls alternately, the leads first, then the skips similarly.

(For other than International and Commonwealth Games, players in a pairs game may play two, three or four bowls each, as previously arranged by the controlling body).

16. A triples game by two contending teams of three players, who shall play two or three bowls singly and in turn, the leads playing first.

17. A fours game by two contending teams of four players, each member playing two bowls single and in turn.

18. A side game shall be played by two contending sides, each composed of an equal number of teams players.

19. Games in series shall be arranged to be played on several and consecutive occasions as:–

(a) A series or sequence of games organised in the form of an eliminating competition, and arranged as singles, pairs, triples or fours.

(b) A series or sequence of side matches organised in the form of a league competition, or an eliminating competition, or of inter-association matches.

20. A special tournament of games:

Single games and team games may also be arranged in group form as a special tournament of games in which the contestants play each other in turn, or they may play as paired off teams of players on one or several greens in accordance with a common time-table, success being adjudged by the number of games won, or by the highest net score in shots in accordance with the regulations governing the Tournament.

21. For International Matches, World Bowls and Commonwealth Games, in matches where played,

(i) Singles shall be 25 shots up (shots in excess of 25 shall not count), four bowls each player, played alternately; *(EBA ruling only: Singles play under EBA jurisdiction shall be 21 shots up)*.

(ii) Pairs shall be 21 ends, four bowls each player, played alternately;

(iii) Triples shall be 18 ends, three bowls each player, played alternately;

(iv) Fours shall be 21 ends, two bowls each player, played alternately;

PROVIDED that pairs, triples and fours may be of a lesser number of ends, but in the case of pairs and fours there shall not be less than 18 ends and in the case of triples not less than 15 ends, subject in all cases to the express approval of the Board as represented by its most senior officer present. If there be no officer of the Board present at the time, the decision shall rest with the "Controlling Body" as defined in Law 1. Any decision to curtail the number of ends to be played shall be made before the commencement of any game, and such decision shall only be made on the grounds of climatic conditions, inclement weather or shortage of time to complete a programme.

22. Awards

Cancelled: see By-Laws after Rule 73 under heading "Professional Bowler".

STARTING THE GAME

23. (a) **Trial ends**

Before start of play in any competition, match or game, or on the resumption of an unfinished competition, match or game on another day, not more than one trial end each way shall be played.

(b) **Tossing for opening play**

The captains in a side game or skips in a team shall toss to decide which side or team shall play first, but in all singles games the opponents shall toss, the winner of the toss to have the option of decision. In the event of a tied (no score) or a dead end, the first to play in the tied end or dead end shall again play first.

In all ends subsequent to the first the winner of the preceding scoring end shall play first.

24. Placing the Mat

At the beginning of the first end the player to play first shall place the mat lengthwise on the centre line of the rink, the back edge of the mat to be six feet from the ditch. (Where ground sheets are in use, the mat at the first and every subsequent end, shall be placed at the back edge of the sheet – the mat's front edge being six feet from the ditch).

25. The Mat and its replacement

After play has commenced in any end the mat shall not be moved from its first position.

If the mat be displaced during the progress of an end it shall be replaced as near as practicable in the same position.

If the mat be out of alignment with the centre line of the rink it may be straightened at any time during the end.

After the last bowl in each end has come to rest in play, or has sooner become dead, the mat shall be lifted and placed wholly beyond the face of the rear bank. Should the mat be picked up by a player before the end has been completed, the opposing player shall have the right of replacing the mat in its original position.

26. The Mat in subsequent ends

(a)

In all subsequent ends the front edge of the mat shall be not less than six feet from the rear ditch and the front edge not less than 76 feet from the front ditch, and on the centre line of the rink of play. *(EBA ruling only: For 76 feet (23.16 metres) read 27 yards (24.69 metres))*.

(b) Should the Jack be improperly delivered under Law 30, the opposing player may then move the mat in the line of play, subject to clause (a) above, and deliver the Jack but shall not play first. Should the Jack be improperly delivered twice by each player in any end it shall not be delivered again in that end, but shall be centred so that the front of the Jack is a distance of six feet from the opposite ditch and the mat placed at the option of the first to play.

If after the Jack is set at a regulation length from the ditch (6 feet, 1.84 metres) and both players each having improperly delivered the Jack twice, that end is then made dead, the winner of the preceding scoring end shall deliver the Jack when the end is played anew.

27. Stance on Mat

A player shall take his stance on the mat, and at the moment of delivering Jack or his Bowl, shall have one foot remaining entirely within the confines of the Mat. The foot may be either in contact with, or over the mat. Failure to observe this law constitutes foot-faulting.

28. Foot-faulting

Should a player infringe the Law of foot-faulting the Umpire may after having given a warning, have the bowl stopped and declared dead. If the bowl has disturbed the head, the opponent shall have the option of either resetting the head, leaving the head as altered or declaring the end dead.

29. Delivering the Jack

The player to play first shall deliver the Jack. If the Jack in its original course comes to rest at a distance of less than 2 yards from the opposite ditch, it shall be moved out to a mark at that distance so that the front of the Jack is six feet (1.84 metres) from the front ditch. *(EBA ruling: If a mark has not been placed on the green, the Jack shall be moved so that the front edge of the Jack is six feet (1.84 metres) from the front ditch and centred.)*

If the Jack during its original course be obstructed or deflected by a neutral object or neutral person, or by a marker, opponent or member of the opposing team, it shall be redelivered by the same player, but if it be obstructed or

Laws of the game

deflected by a member of his own team, it shall be redelivered by the Lead of the opposing team who shall be entitled to re-set the mat.

30. Jack improperly delivered

Should the jack in any end be not delivered from a proper stance on the mat, or if it ends its original course in the ditch or outside the side boundary of the rink, or less than 70 feet in a straight line of play from the front edge of the mat, it shall be returned and the opposing player shall deliver the Jack but shall not play first. *(EBA ruling: for 70 feet read 25 yards (22.86 metres))*.

The Jack shall be returned if it is improperly delivered, but the right of the player first delivering the Jack in that end, to play the first bowl of the end shall not be affected.

No player shall be permitted to challenge the legality of the original length of the Jack after each player in a singles game or leads in a team game have each bowled one bowl.

31. Variations to Laws 24, 26, 29 and 30

Notwithstanding anything contained in Laws 24, 26, 29 and 30, any National Authority may for domestic purposes, but not in any International Matches, World Bowls Championships or Commonwealth Games, vary any of the distances mentioned in these Laws.

MOVEMENT OF BOWLS

32. "Live" Bowl

A Bowl, which in its original course on the Green, comes to rest within the boundaries of the rink, and not less than 15 yards from the front edge of the mat, shall be accounted as a "Live" bowl and shall be in play.

33. "Touchers"

A bowl which in its original course on the green, touches the Jack, even though such bowl passes into the ditch within the boundaries of the rink shall be counted as a "live" bowl and shall be called a "toucher". If after having come to rest a bowl falls over and touches the Jack before the next succeeding bowl is delivered, or if in the case of the last bowl of an end it falls and touches the Jack within the period of half-minute invoked under Law 53, such bowl shall also be a "toucher". No bowl shall be accounted a "toucher" by playing on to, or by coming into contact with the Jack while the Jack is in the ditch. If a "toucher" in the ditch cannot be seen from the mat its position may be marked by a white or coloured peg about 2 inches broad placed upright on the top of the bank and immediately in line with the place where the "toucher" rests.

34. Marking a "Toucher"

A "toucher" shall be clearly marked with a chalk mark by a member of the player's team. If, in the opinion of either Skip, or opponent in Singles, a "toucher" or a wrongly chalked bowl comes to rest in such a position that the act of making a chalk mark, or of erasing it, is likely to move the bowl or to alter the head, the bowl shall not be marked or have its mark erased but shall be "indicated" as a "toucher" or "non-toucher" as the case may be. If a bowl is not so marked or not so "indicated" before the succeeding bowl comes to rest it ceases to be a "toucher". If both Skips or opponents agree that any subsequent movement of the bowl eliminates the necessity for continuation of the "indicated" provision the bowl shall thereupon be marked or have the chalk mark erased as the case may be. Care should be taken to remove "toucher" marks from all bowls before they are played, but should a

player fail to do so, and should the bowl not become a "toucher" in the end in play, the marks shall be removed by the opposing Skip or his deputy or marker immediately the bowl comes to rest unless the bowl is "indicated" as a "non-toucher" in circumstances governed by earlier provisions of this Law.

35. Movement of "Touchers"

A "toucher" in play in the ditch may be moved by the impact of a jack in play or of another "toucher" in play, and also by the impact of a non-toucher which remains in play after the impact, and any movement of the "toucher" by such incidents shall be valid. However, should the non-toucher enter the ditch at any time after the impact, it shall be dead, and the "toucher" shall be deemed to have been displaced by a dead bowl and the provisions of Law 38(e) shall apply.

36. Bowl Accounted "Dead"

(a) Without limiting the application of any other of these Laws, a bowl shall be accounted dead if it:
　(i) not being a "toucher", comes to rest in the ditch or rebounds on to the playing surface of the rink after contact with the bank or with the Jack or a "toucher" in the ditch, or
　(ii) after completing its original course, or after being moved as a result of play, it comes to rest wholly outside the boundaries of the playing surface of the rink, or within 15 yards of the front of the mat, or
　(iii) in its original course, pass beyond a side boundary of the rink on a bias which would prevent its re-entering the rink. (A bowl is not rendered "dead" by a player carrying it whilst inspecting the head).

(b) Skips, or Opponents in Singles, shall agree on the question as to whether or not a bowl is "dead", and having reached agreement, the question shall not later by subject to appeal to the Umpire. Any member of either team may request a decision from the Skips but no member shall remove any bowl prior to the agreement of the Skips. If Skips or Opponents are unable to reach agreement as to whether or not a bowl is "dead" the matter shall be referred to the Umpire.

37. Bowl Rebounding

Only "Touchers" rebounding from the face of the bank to the ditch or to the rink shall remain in play.

38. Bowl displacement

(a) Displacement by rebounding "non-toucher" – bowl displaced by a "non-toucher" rebounding from the bank shall be restored as near as possible to its original position, by a member of the opposing team.

(b) Displacement by participating player – if a bowl, while in motion or at rest on the green or a "toucher" in the ditch, be interfered with, or displaced by one of the players, the opposing skip shall have the option of:
　(i) restoring the bowl as near as possible to its original position;
　(ii) letting it remain where it rests;
　(iii) declaring the bowl "dead";
　(iv) or declaring the end dead.

(c) Displacement by a neutral object or neutral person

59. Playing to a finish and possible drawn games

If in an eliminating competition, consisting of a stated or agreed upon number of ends, it be found, when all the ends have been played, that the scores are equal, an extra end or ends shall be played until a decision has been reached.

The captains or skips shall toss and the winner shall have the right to decide who shall play first. The extra end shall be played from where the previous end was completed, and the mat shall be placed in accordance with Law 24.

DEFAULTS OF PLAYERS IN FOURS PLAY

60. Absentee players in any team or side

(a) **In a single fours game,** for a trophy, prize or other competitive award, where a club is represented by only one four, each member of such four shall be a bona-fide member of the club. Unless all four players appear and are ready to play at the end of the maximum waiting period of 30 minutes, or should they introduce an ineligible player, then that team shall forfeit the match to the opposing team.

(b) **In a domestic fours game.** Where, in a domestic fours game the number of players cannot be accommodated in full teams of four players, three players may play against three players, but shall suffer the deduction of one fourth of the total score of each team.

A smaller number of players than six shall be excluded from that game.

(c) **In a Side game.** If within a period of 30 minutes from the time fixed for the game, a single player is absent from one or both teams in a side game, whether a friendly club match or a match for a trophy, prize or other award, the game shall proceed, but in the defaulting team, the number of bowls shall be made up by the lead and second players playing three bowls each, but one-fourth of the total shots scored by each "four" playing three men shall be deducted from their score at the end of the game. Fractions shall be taken into account.

(d) **In a Side game.** Should such default take place where more fours than one are concerned, or where a four has been disqualified for some other infringement, and where the average score is to decide the contest, the scores of the non-defaulting fours only shall be counted, but such average shall, as a penalty in the case of the defaulting side, be arrived at by dividing the aggregate score of that side by the number of fours that should have been played and not as in the case of the other side, by the number actually engaged in the game.

61. Play irregularities

(a) **Playing out of turn.** When a player has played before his turn the opposing skip shall have the right to stop the bowl in its course and it shall be played in its proper turn, but in the event of the bowl so played, having moved or displaced the jack or bowl, the opposing skip shall have the option of allowing the end to remain as it is after the bowl so played, has come to rest, or having the end declared "dead".

(b) **Playing the wrong bowl.** A bowl played by mistake shall be replaced by the player's own bowl.

(c) **Changing bowls.** A player shall not be allowed to change his bowls during the course of a game, or in a

resumed game, unless they be objected to, as provided in Law 9(c), or when a bowl has been so damaged in the course of play as, in the opinion of the Umpire, to render the bowl unit for play.

(d) **Omitting to play.**

(i) If the result of an end has been agreed upon, or the head has been touched in the agreed process of determining the result, then a player who forfeits or has omitted to play a bowl, shall forfeit the right to play it.

(ii) A player who has neglected to play a bowl in the proper sequence shall forfeit the right to play such bowl, if a bowl has been played by each team before such mistake was discovered.

(iii) If before the mistake be noticed, a bowl has been delivered in the reversed order and the head has not been disturbed, the opponent shall then play two successive bowls to restore the correct sequence. If the head has been disturbed Clause 61(a) shall apply.

62. Play Interruptions

(a) **Game Stoppages.** When a game of any kind is stopped, either by mutual arrangement or by the Umpire, after appeal to him on account of darkness or the conditions of the weather, or any other valid reason, it shall be resumed with the scores as they were when the game stopped. An end commenced, but not completed, shall be declared null.

(b) **Substitutes in a resumed game.** If in a resumed game any one of the four original players be not available, one substitute shall be permitted as stated in Law 63 below. Players, however, shall not be transferred from one team to another.

63. Leaving the Green

If during the course of a side fours, triples or pairs game a player has to leave the green owing to illness, or other reasonable cause, his place shall be filled by a substitute, if in the opinion of both skips (or failing agreement by them, then in the opinion of the Controlling Body) such substitution is necessary. Should the player affected be a skip, his duties and position in a fours game shall be assumed by the third player, and the substitute shall play either as a lead, second or third. In the case of Triples the substitute may play either as lead or second but not as skip and in the case of Pairs the substitute shall play as lead only. Such substitute shall be a member of the club to which the team belongs. In domestic play National Associations may decide the position of any substitute.

If during the course of a single-handed game, a player has to leave the green owing to illness, or reasonable cause, the provision of Law 62(a) shall be observed.

No player shall be allowed to delay the play by leaving the rink or team, unless with the consent of his opponent, and then only for a period not exceeding ten minutes.

Contravention of this Law shall entitle the opponent or opposing team to claim the game or match.

64. Objects on the Green

Under no circumstances, other than as provided in Laws 33 and 40 shall any extraneous object to assist a player be placed on the green, or on the bank, or on the jack, or on a bowl or elsewhere.

65. Unforeseen incidents

If during the course of play, the position of the jack or bowls be disturbed by wind, storm, or by any neutral object the end shall be declared "dead", unless the skips are agreed as to the replacement of jack or bowls.

DOMESTIC ARRANGEMENTS

66. In addition to any matters specifically mentioned in these Laws, National Associations may, in circumstances dictated by climate or other local conditions, make such other regulations as are deemed necessary and desirable, but such regulations must be submitted to the I.B.B. for approval. For this purpose the Board shall appoint a Committee to be known as the "Laws Committee" with powers to grant approval or otherwise to any proposal, such decision being valid until the proposal is submitted to the Board for a final decision.

67. Local Arrangements

Constituent clubs of National Associations shall also in making their domestic arrangements make such regulations as are deemed necessary to govern their club competitions, but such regulations shall comply with the Laws of the Game, and be approved by the Council of their National Association.

68. National Visiting Teams or Sides

No team or side of bowlers visiting overseas or the British Isles shall be recognised by the International Bowling Board unless it first be sanctioned and recommended by the National Association to which its members are affiliated.

69. Contracting out

No club or club management committee or any individual shall have the right or power to contract out of any of the Laws of the Game as laid down by the IBB.

70. The foregoing laws, where applicable, shall also apply to single-handed, pairs and triples games.

71. Persons not engaged in the Game shall be situated clear of and beyond the limits of the rink of play, and clear of verges. They shall preserve an attitude of strict neutrality, and neither by word nor act disturb or advise the players.

Betting or gambling in connection with any game or games shall not be permitted or engaged in within the grounds of any constituent club.

DUTIES OF MARKER

72. (a) The Marker shall control the game in accordance with the I.B.B. Basic Laws. He shall, before play commences, examine all bowls for the imprint of the I.B.B. Stamp, or that of its National Association, such imprint to be clearly visible, and shall ascertain by measurement the width of the rink of play (see note after Law 73).

(b) He shall centre the jack, and shall place a full length jack two yards from the ditch.

(c) He shall ensure that the Jack is not less than 70 feet from the front edge of the mat, after it has been centred. *(EBA ruling: For 70 feet read 25 yards)*.

(d) He shall stand at one side of the rink, and to the rear of the jack.

(e) He shall answer affirmatively or negatively a player's inquiry as to whether a bowl is jack high. If requested, he shall indicate the distance of any bowl from the jack, or from any other bowl, and also, if requested indicate which bowl he thinks is shot and/or the relative position of any other bowl.

(f) Subject to contrary directions from either opponent under Law 34, he shall mark all touchers immediately they come to rest, and remove chalk marks from non-touchers. With the agreement of both opponents he shall remove all dead bowls from the green and the ditch. He shall mark the positions of the jack and touchers which are in the ditch. (See Laws 33 and 40).

(g) He shall not move, or cause to be moved, either jack or bowls until each players has agreed to the number of shots.

(h) He shall measure carefully all doubtful shots when requested by either player. If unable to come to a decision satisfactory to the players, he shall call in an Umpire. If an official Umpire has not been appointed, the marker shall select one. The decision of the Umpire shall be final.

(i) He shall enter the score at each end, and shall intimate to the players the state of the game. When the game is finished, he shall see that the score card, containing the names of the players, is signed by the players, and disposed of in accordance with the rules of the competition.

DUTIES OF UMPIRE

73. An Umpire shall be appointed by the Controlling Body of the Association, Club or Tournament Management Committee. His duties shall be as follows:

(a) He shall examine all bowls for the imprint of the I.B.B. Stamp, or that of its National Association, and ascertain by measurement the width of the rinks of play.

(b) He shall measure any shot or shots in dispute, and for this purpose shall use a suitable measure. His decision shall be final.

(c) He shall decide all questions as to the distance of the mat from the ditch, and the jack from the mat.

(d) He shall decide as to whether or not jack and/or bowls are in play.

(e) He shall enforce the Laws of the Game.

(f) In World Bowls Championships and Commonwealth Games, the umpire's decision shall be final in respect of any breach of a Law, except that, upon questions relating to the meaning or interpretation of any Law there shall be a right of appeal to the controlling body.

NOTE

International Bowling Board by-laws include the following:

PROFESSIONAL BOWLER

All players are elligible for selection for Commonwealth Games except those whose principal income is derived from playing the game of bowls.

STAMPING OF BOWLS

Each bowl complying with Law 9 shall bear the official stamp of the Board. Currency shall be for a period of 15 years expiring on December 31 and the imprint shall record the latest year in which such bowl may be validly used. *(The 15 years referred to is a BIBC decision for domestic play only)*.

Any member national authority may make its own arrangements for testing and stamping of bowls and such bowls shall be valid for play in all matches controlled by that authority. Provided that bowls comply with law 9 of the Board's Laws as amended and bear a current stamp of the Board and/or a member national authority and/or the BIBC, such bowls may be used for International, Commonwealth or World championship matches.